AF248761

THE SECRET HISTORY OF FOOD

BY SUSAN TOMNAY

ILLUSTRATED BY NADINE WICKENDEN

CONTENTS

CHAPTER ONE

FOOD AND CULTURE

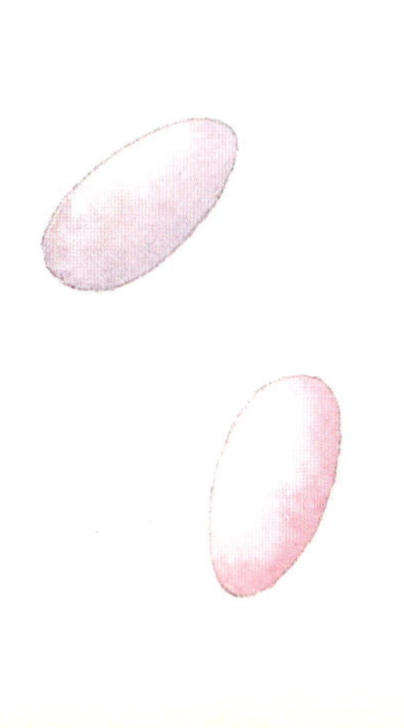

FOOD IS ONE OF OUR MOST POWERFUL SYMBOLS OF LOVE — just ask anyone who has ever made a special dinner for a loved one. First you decide what to serve, adding this, discarding that, until you come up with the perfect menu. Then the table — what flowers should you buy? Are there to be candles? There's the time spent shopping and the actual preparation — can anything be done in advance? You want to be in the kitchen as little as possible while your guest is with you, so the whole thing has to be worked out with military precision. At last you serve the meal: and it's a gift of your self — your creativity, your time, your care, your love.

Even an everyday family meal requires thought and time, regard for nutrition and family members' preferences. Food cooked with love is food cooked with care — and you can taste it. For most of us, sharing food is the centre of family life. Food is what brings us together. We cook up celebratory feasts for family at Christmas and on birthdays, friends are invited for meals as a social occasion and even an unexpected visitor will be offered a cup of coffee or tea. Sharing our food is our major way of showing hospitality. This is, and has always been, true of every culture.

OUR RELATIONSHIP WITH FOOD has gone beyond simply eating to sustain life. Used for showing hospitality, for marking special events and rites of passage, food is also one of the things that we turn to in times of stress. This is so much the case that food addiction has become a major problem in the West, and organisations such as Overeaters Anonymous have been set up in a number of countries to help people to control their compulsive eating.

At the other end of the scale, anorexia nervosa is thought to be associated with feelings of lack of control — hunger strikes have always been the last resort of the powerless.

A food craving is a different thing from food addiction. A compulsive eater will eat anything that's available, whereas a craving is for a specific kind of food. It might be for a food group such as carbohydrates or it might for be for salty food, or more commonly, for chocolate. If your diet is normally healthy and well balanced, giving in to a food craving is probably sensible. Your body may be telling you that it needs specific nutrients, or perhaps, in the case of chocolate, that you just need some comfort.

THROUGHOUT THE CENTURIES, food has been a central theme in fables and folklore. Generations of children have been brought up on nursery rhymes featuring food: The Queen of Hearts, She made some tarts...; Sugar and spice and all things nice.... And this one, expressing deep satisfaction in the symbiosis between husband and wife:

Jack Spratt could eat no fat,

His wife could eat no lean,

And so between them both, you see,

They licked the platter clean.

In one of Aesop's best known fables, *The Ants and the Grasshopper*, food is used is to stress the importance of future planning:

One fine winter day some ants were drying off their store of corn which had become wet during a storm. Along came a grasshopper and begged for some food for, he said, he was starving. 'What were you doing with yourself last summer?' said the ants. 'I was busy singing,' said the grasshopper. 'Well, you'd better spend the winter dancing,' said the pitiless ants.

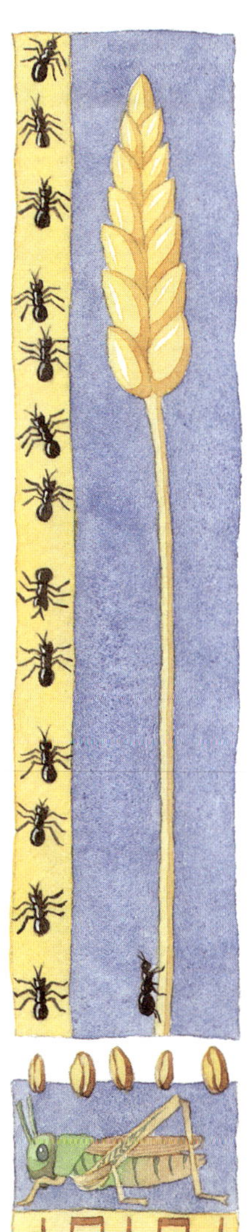

NEARLY ALL OUR TIMES OF CELEBRATION and rites of passage are marked by feasts and special foods — in modern life there aren't many rituals left so we cling all the more tightly to those few that remain to us. Roast turkey is essential Christmas fare, so much so that it is even eaten in the southern hemisphere when Christmas falls in the middle of summer. Christmas pudding, Christmas cake and mince pies are really only eaten once a year, and that's part of what makes them so special.

The food served at times of celebration is, in many ways, as important as the actual occasion that is being celebrated, the two are inextricably linked. Christmas wouldn't be Christmas without the mince pies and Christmas pudding, just as in the USA Thanksgiving wouldn't be Thanksgiving without the turkey, chestnut stuffing, and pumpkin pie, and Halloween would be something else altogether without the pumpkin!

At Christmas, Queen Victoria had quantities of raised pies made in her kitchens, to be sent out as gifts to her friends. Each pie contained four birds: a woodcock, pheasant, chicken and turkey. They were all boned and then the woodcock was placed inside the pheasant, the pheasant inside the chicken and the chicken inside the turkey. The whole lot was packed into a pie dish, the gaps were filled with a stuffing of forcemeat, truffles and tongue, and topped with rich pastry. Each slice of pie would contain a taste of the four birds.

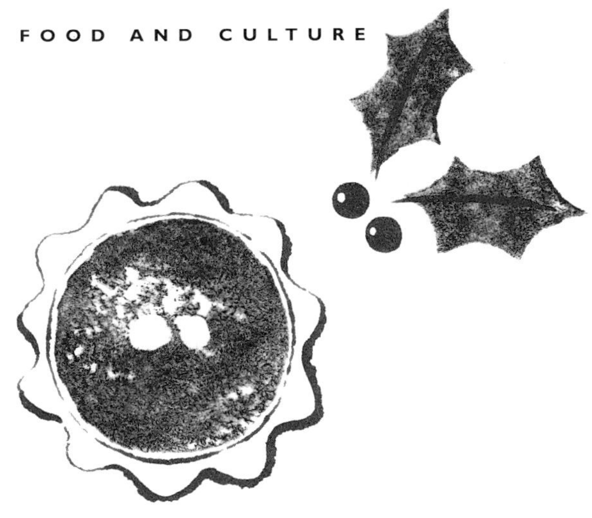

I N ELIZABETHAN ENGLAND, mince pies made with minced meat, dried fruit and brandy were popular at Christmas, as was an interesting concoction known as plum porridge. They went out of fashion during the seventeenth century but were taken up again with gusto after the Restoration. Mrs Beeton's 1861 recipe for mincemeat includes raw minced rump steak and it is still praised for its excellent flavour and good keeping qualities by cookery writers today. In England, meat was eliminated from mince pies by the 1930s, although at this time American mincemeat still contained cooked beef.

A Recipe for Plum Porridge

Traditional Christmas fare in 16th, 17th and 18th-century England.

'Put a leg and shin of beef into eight gallons of water, and boil them till they be very tender. When the broth be strong, strain it out. Then wipe the pot and put in the broth again. Slice six penny loaves thin, cut off the tops and bottoms, put some of the liquor to them and cover them up and let them stand for a quarter of an hour; then boil and strain it, and put it into your pot. Let it boil a quarter of an hour, then put in five pounds of currants, clean washed and picked. Let them boil a little, and then put in five pounds of stoned raisins of the sun, and two pounds of prunes. Let these boil till they swell, and then put in three quarters of an ounce of mace, half an ounce of cloves, and two nutmegs, all beat fine. Before you put these into the pot, mix them with a little cold liquor and do not put them in but a little while before you take off the pot. When you take off the pot, put in three pounds of sugar, a little salt, a quart of sack [dry white wine], a quart of claret, and the juice of two or three lemons. You may thicken with sago instead of bread if you please. Pour your porridge into earthen pans and keep it for use.'

PLUM PORRIDGE FOR CHRISTMAS

THE LONDON ART OF COOKERY, BY JOHN FARLEY, 1783

THE FIRST ENGLISH WEDDING CAKE was a round, flat spicy cake which was broken over the bride's head, symbolising the end of her maidenhood. Today the traditional English wedding cake is a rich, dark fruit cake, covered with marzipan and then coated with royal icing. The tradition of the bride and groom cutting the cake together arose because the icing was so hard, the bride needed help to cut through it! The cake is often constructed in three tiers, with sugar pillars in between.

The top tier is usually not cut at the wedding, but carefully wrapped and stored, to be eaten either at the couple's first anniversary or at the christening of their first child. In the past, young unmarried women didn't eat their slice of cake, but slept with it under their pillow. It was meant to ensure that they too, would soon meet their own true love. American wedding cakes are usually much lighter — sponge cakes, butter cakes or cheesecakes. They are iced and decorated but are not meant for keeping and certainly not for placing under the pillow. A portion of the cake is frozen if it's to be kept for the first anniversary.

In France, wedding cakes aren't as much of a tradition as they are in England and America. When a French bride does have a wedding cake, it's more often than not a croquembouche — an elegant cone-shaped structure made out of little choux puffs, decorated with spun sugar, sugared almonds and sugar flowers.

THE ETIQUETTE AS WELL AS THE TRADITIONS surrounding food vary between countries and cultures. When you bring flowers to a dinner party as a gift for your host, you must be careful — not only are flowers themselves symbolic (red roses indicate love), but they have different meanings in different cultures. In Bulgaria if you gave yellow roses, your host might think that you dislike her. Some flowers, lilies and chrysanthemums in particular, are traditionally seen at funerals, and might not be appropriate at dinner. Avoid giving highly perfumed flowers such as tuberoses or violets as your host may feel obliged to display your flowers on the table and the strong scent could put people off their food.

Bringing a bottle of wine to dinner also has its dangers. A host in Italy, Portugal or Spain might see it as an affront — a suggestion that they can't afford enough wine for the dinner. It also puts the host in a quandary — should they serve your wine at dinner, even though they have thoughtfully chosen the wines for the meal (especially if yours is inferior)? Or should they risk offending you by putting your wine aside?

If you salt your food before tasting it

you run the risk of offending your host who

may have gone to considerable trouble to season

the dish perfectly — in Hungary this is considered

most impolite.

But it raises a problem: if you taste your dinner

and then reach for the salt cellar, are you not indicating

that the food is not sufficiently seasoned? In China,

if you add salt to your food, you may

well find your host apologising

profusely to you.

IN POLITE SOCIETY it has always been considered correct to put the milk in a cup of tea after the tea is poured, never before. In fact the phrase 'rather MIF' (milk in first) has been used to describe people who don't quite fit in.

Connoisseurs of tea, however, insist that tea tastes better if the milk is poured into the cup first. It has a more blended

taste because the milk 'cooks' slightly when the hot tea is poured over it. When cream is offered instead of milk (usually with coffee — although in the past cream was often added to tea), it is added last because the hot liquid poured over the cream would scald it and spoil its flavour. So you have a dilemma: is it to be good breeding or good taste?

HOW YOU SHOW YOUR APPRECIATION of a meal varies widely between cultures. In the United States, Britain, Australia and most of Europe, a murmur of approval when the food is set upon the table is all that is required. Being over-exuberant in your praise might look as if you are surprised or relieved that the food is good. Or it might be taken as a not-so-subtle hint that you want some more. It is also impolite in Western society (or was, until fairly recently) to discuss food while you're eating. In her 1778 novel, *Evelina*, Fanny Burney's heroine is disgusted when 'men of rank and fashion' talk about food and cooking while at dinner. It was considered very bad form in polite circles right up to the First World War. The rules have slowly relaxed since then and now, particularly in restaurants, you find people eagerly discussing the food they are eating, food they have eaten in the past and food they intend to eat. Even recipes

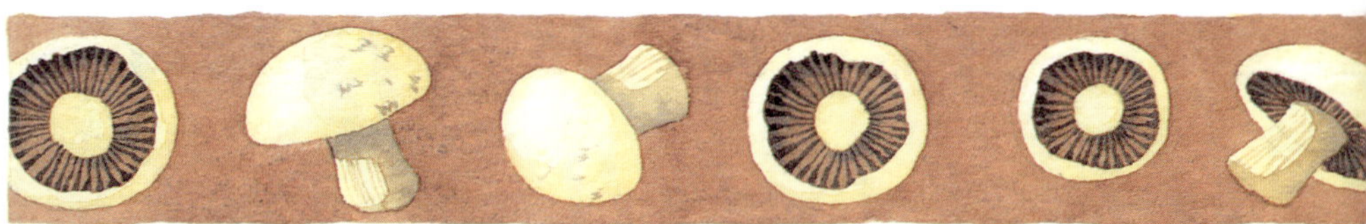

are exchanged — something that women always did in private in the past, for fear of boring the men, and of appearing too domestic. At a Chinese banquet, however, guests are expected to be unstinting in their praise of the food, and in some cultures, especially those of the Pacific Islands, a loud belch adequately expresses your appreciation!

'Whatever may be your inclination, cautiously abstain from being helped a second time from the same dish: a man's character has been damned in society in consequence of being stigmatised as "one of those fellows who call twice for soup!"'

LAUNCELOT STURGEON,
THE IMPORTANCE OF GOOD LIVING, 1822

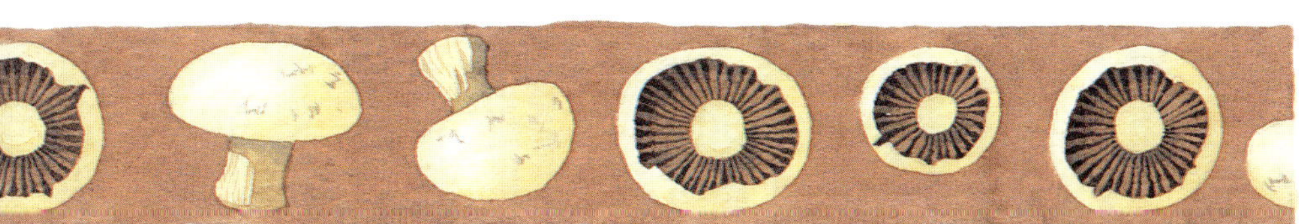

CHAPTER TWO

THE UNTOLD HISTORY

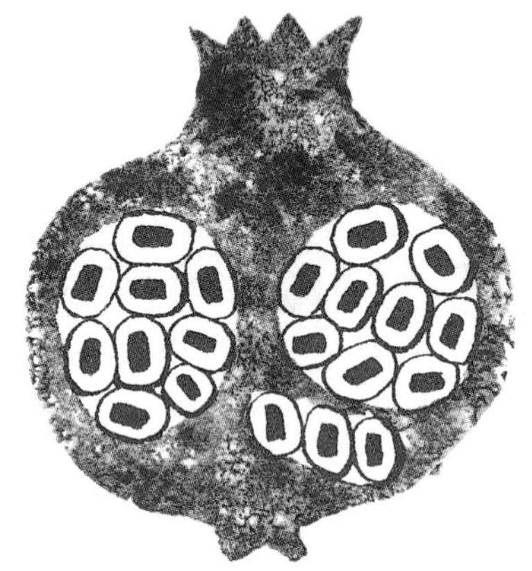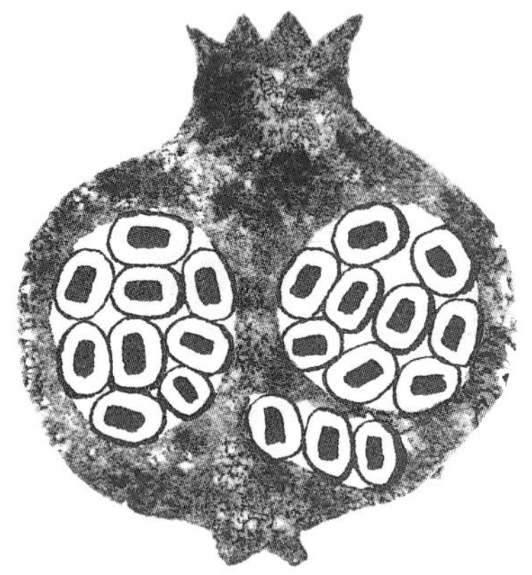

DEMETER THE GODDESS OF AGRICULTURE had a much-loved daughter, Persephone, who was abducted by Hades and taken to the underworld. Demeter searched for a long time for Persephone and while she did, the earth was barren and the people went hungry.

Finally Demeter's brother Zeus, who had plotted with Hades to capture Persephone, sent a message for him to release her. Hades did this reluctantly, but at the last minute, when Persephone wasn't looking, he popped a pomegranate seed

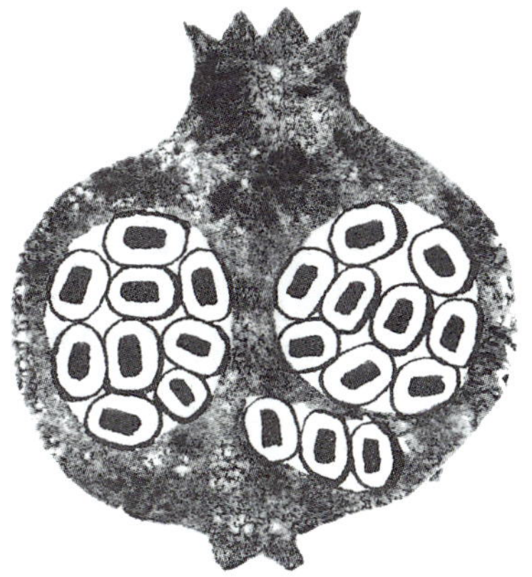 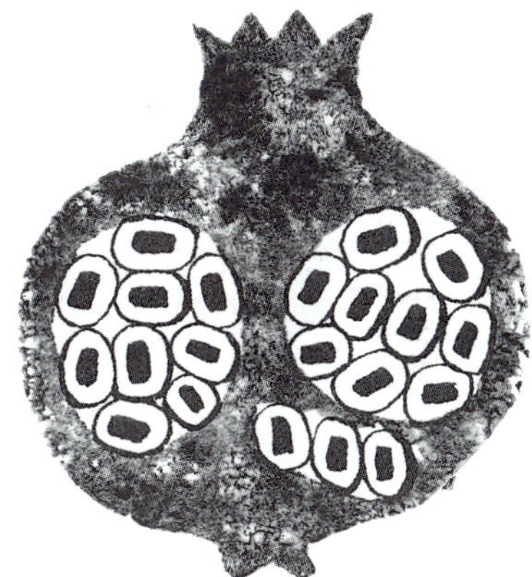

into her mouth, thus ensuring her return. (If you eat the food of the underworld, you must return to it.) When Persephone and Demeter were reunited, the earth became rich again with flowers and fruit and grain.

But Persephone could only spend nine months of the year above ground, the remaining three months she had to spend in the underworld. In the nine months above ground — Spring, Summer and Autumn — the earth is fruitful; in the winter it lies dormant, waiting for Persephone's return.

IN ANCIENT GREECE THE PHILOSOPHER, ARISTOXENON,

sprinkled the lettuces in his garden with wine and honey in

the evening. He picked them next day at dawn and ate them

with their ready made dressing, calling them 'green cakes', given

to him by the earth.

IN ANCIENT GREECE THERE WAS A

GENTLEMAN NAMED PITHYLLOS, CALLED

PITHYLLOS THE PICKY BY HIS FRIENDS,

WHO KEPT HIS TONGUE IN A BAG

BETWEEN MEALS IN ORDER TO PRESERVE

ITS SENSITIVITY.

W HEN THE ANCIENT GREEKS went to the polls to vote, they wrote down on flat oyster shells (ostrakons) the names of people they felt should be banished as not suitable to hold a position of power. That's how the word 'ostracism' came about.

Our delicate servings of a half-dozen or dozen oysters would seem ridiculously paltry to the oyster lovers of the past. The Roman statesman and orator Seneca (c. 4BC-AD65) is said to have swallowed one hundred dozen oysters every week. Henry IV of France (1553-1610) liked to eat 300 oysters to sharpen his appetite for dinner, and at the time of Louis XIV (1638-1715), there were about 2000 oyster sellers in Paris. Oysters were cheap and plentiful in England, Europe and America until the late nineteenth century. In England they were regarded as the food of the poor, with pickled oysters being particularly popular in Victorian England.

In America there's evidence from the heaps of shells found that the American Indians enjoyed oysters long before white settlement — one mound in Maine, is estimated to contain seven million bushels. Captain John Smith noted the enormous number of oysters to be found on American shores and their large size, and Charles Dickens on his visit to America in 1842 described New York's numerous oyster-cellars. By the end of the nineteenth century America and Europe started running out of oysters and prices began to rise. They have never been thought of as 'poor food' since.

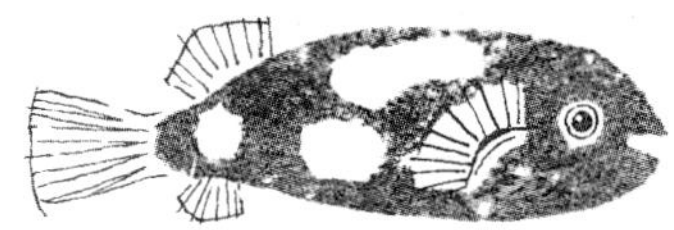

ONE LEGEND OF HOW PASTA came to be invented goes like this: a young man named Chicco, who lived in Naples at the time of King Frederick II, spent every day in his room perfecting a secret new recipe. One of his neighbours, Giovannella, spied on him through the keyhole. One day as she was watching him, Chicco gave a great shout of delight — he had discovered pasta. Giovannella stole Chicco's recipe and cooked the dish for the king. The king loved the pasta and soon people were paying Giovannella for the recipe. Meanwhile Chicco disappeared, heartbroken at the theft of his recipe.

Giovannella became very rich, but it wasn't long before she sickened and died. Legend has it that Chicco comes back every Saturday night to the house where he first made his discovery, and makes pasta, while Giovannella ceaselessly stirs the sauce and the Devil blows on the fire to keep it burning.

TORQUATO TASSO (1544-1595) the Italian poet tells the story of how tortellini came to be invented. It seems that the goddess Venus was wandering around Bologna and stopped at an inn for the night. The innkeeper, smitten by her beauty, couldn't stop himself from spying on her through the keyhole of her bedroom door. Unfortunately for him, all he could see of her nakedness was her navel. But he was so inspired that he went back to the kitchen and created tortellini — an edible homage to that magnificent navel.

TRENCHERS OR PLATES MADE FROM BREAD were used at medieval banquets. Thick slices of unleavened wholewheat bread, about four days old, were cut into squares or rectangles and diners placed their meat and thickened sauce on them. At the end of the meal, the trenchers, which by now were soaked with meat juices, might be eaten or given to the poor along with other leftover food. In the fifteenth century, bread trenchers were gradually replaced by wooden ones. By the end of the seventeenth century, flat ceramic plates were fairly common in France. But the change from wooden trenchers to pewter or china plates was quite slow in America — they weren't in common use until the beginning of the nineteenth century.

Here is a list of the food purchased for a royal banquet given by

King Richard II in 1387. Note the complete absence of vegetables!

14 salted oxen	50 swans	1200 pigeons
2 fresh oxen	210 geese	96 young rabbits
120 fresh sheeps' heads	50 larded capons	120 curlews
120 fresh sheep carcasses	96 other capons	144 whimbrels
12 boars	720 hens	12 cranes
14 calves	200 pairs of grown rabbits	Sufficient wild fowl
140 pigs	4 pheasants	120 gallons cream
300 marrow bones	5 herons and bitterns	40 gallons curds
Sufficient lard and fat	6 kids	3 bushels of apples
3 tons of salt venison	60 chickens for jelly	11,000 eggs
3 tons of fresh venison	144 chickens to roast	

WHEN THE FIRST TURKEYS were brought to Europe from the New World (thought to be at the end of the fifteenth century) they were taken up with enthusiasm. This was unusual, as most new foods were regarded with suspicion; some — like the tomato — took a couple of centuries to gain favour.

Because of their large size, turkeys were custom-made for feasts, and especially for Christmas. Their golden colour when roasted also added to their appeal — people have always been attracted to gold food for feast days. By 1570, the turkey had usurped the goose as the main course at the Christmas table. In America, there were thousands of wild turkeys when the Europeans arrived; they were so easy to catch that Indian children were given the job of doing it.

The Pilgrims ate wild turkey at the first Thanksgiving, and it has kept its place ever since as the centrepiece of both Thanksgiving and Christmas dinners.

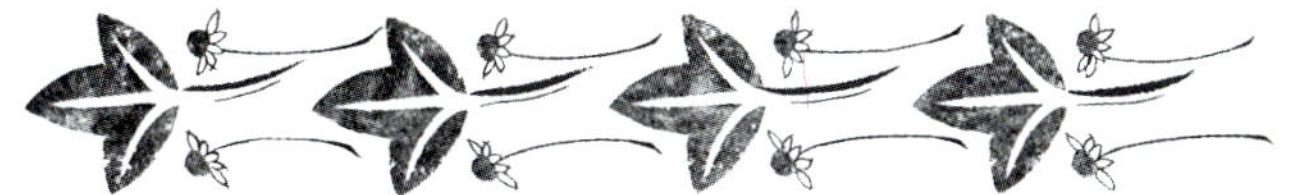

In the late sixteenth century, King Henry IV of France set about restoring his country after 30 years of civil war. One of his main aims was the improvement of agriculture, and he hoped that this would in turn improve the standard of living of the poor. His most famous statement was: 'I hope to make France so prosperous that every peasant will have a chicken in his pot on Sundays.'

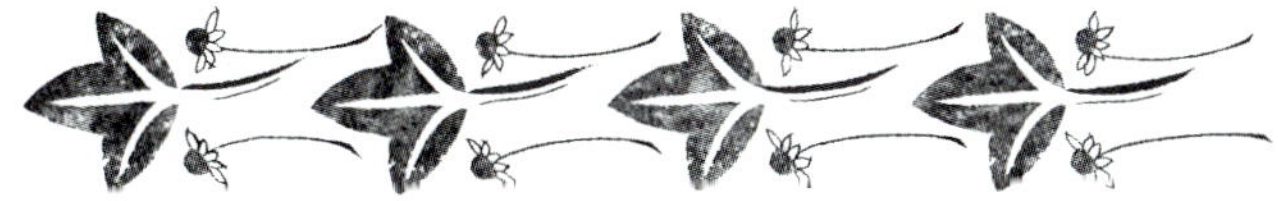

F RENCH CUISINE IS THOUGHT TO HAVE BEGUN IN EARNEST when Catherine de' Medici married the future Henry II of France in 1533. She brought her Florentine chefs with her and they taught Italian gastronomical secrets to French chefs.

Historians who have looked at the cooking of both countries at this time are inclined to doubt that the Italians exerted any great influence over the food of France — it should be noted however, that many of these historians are French. What no one disputes is that the Italians introduced certain refinements to the French court.

One of them was hygiene: washing hands before eating became normal practice. Probably the greatest Italian innovation was the introduction of the fork. At first it was used only to move food from serving dish to trencher; it wasn't until the reign of Henry and Catherine's son, Henry III, that forks began to be used rather than fingers at mealtimes. Italian chefs excelled in constructing sugar desserts and in making sweets, preserves and fruit pastes — dishes previously unknown in France.

MANY CULTURES HAVE EMPLOYED FOOD TASTERS OVER THE CENTURIES, ESPECIALLY FOR THEIR KINGS AND QUEENS. AT MEDIEVAL BANQUETS THE SALT WAS ALWAYS TASTED AS WELL AS THE FOOD — IT WAS THOUGHT THAT POISON COULD BE EASILY INTRODUCED INTO THE SALT CELLAR. IN JAPAN, THE CUSTOM OF TASTING FOOD BEFORE EVERY ROYAL MEAL WAS ONLY OFFICIALLY HALTED IN 1989.

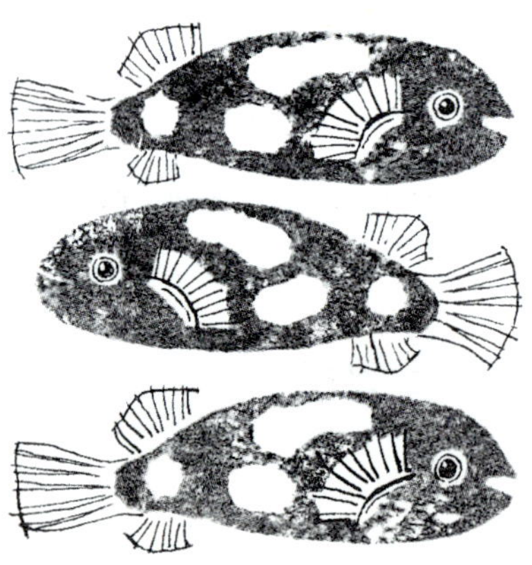

N SEVENTEENTH-CENTURY VERSAILLES, during the reign of Louis XIV, the distance between the kitchen and dining area was about a quarter of a mile. The King's food was carried in procession with an armed guard. The food was covered to keep it as warm as possible on its long journey and to foil would-be poisoners. Despite all these precautions, when now lukewarm food reached the King's table it still had to be tasted by the official taster before he could eat it.

The King usually had his dinner at about 2pm and it was always a public affair, with people coming to watch him eat. Louis XIV was a prodigious eater, a typical meal consisted of four different soups, a pheasant, partridge, chicken or duck, salad, mutton, ham, pastries, fruit, compotes and preserves. When his body was examined after his death, he was found to have an enormous stomach and bowels twice the usual length.

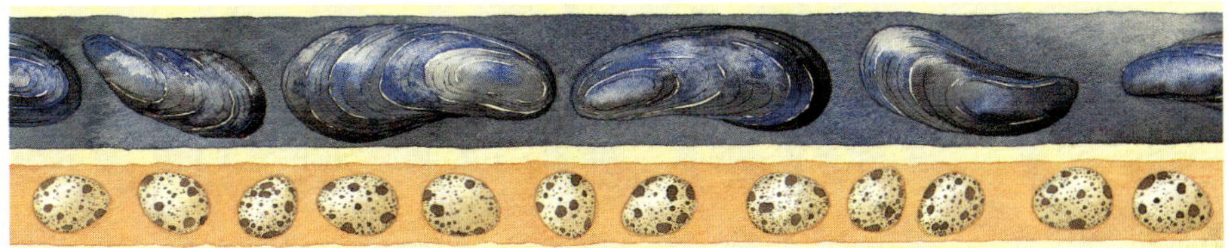

THE FIRST CAFÉS WERE OPENED IN PARIS in the late seventeenth century when the lemonade sellers started a guild, the *Compagnie des Limonadiers*, to prevent 'just anyone' from selling lemonade. Before the formation of this guild, lemonade sellers had walked the streets, carrying the drink on their backs in metal containers, but now they began to open little shops selling coffee and chocolate, and the café was born. Until the middle of the nineteenth century, café owners in Paris were known as limonadiers.

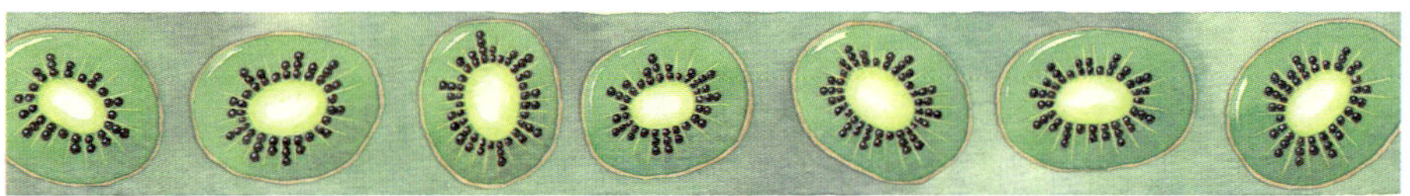

One of the most successful limonadiers of Paris was Procopio dei Coltelli, an Italian who started his working life in Paris as a waiter. Soon he heard about the burgeoning coffee houses of Vienna and decided that Paris was ready for a real café. In 1686 he opened *Café Procope* in the rue des Fosses-Saint-Germain. It was luxuriously appointed with mirrors and crystal chandeliers. The news of the day was pinned to the stovepipe, there were chess sets, and best of all there was coffee, chocolate, liqueurs, aperitif wines, conserved fruit, sherbets and Viennese ices.

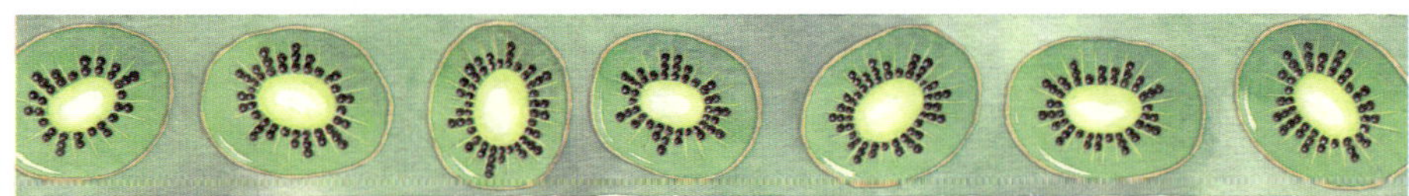

F YOU'VE EVER WONDERED WHO IT WAS WHO DISCOVERED THAT A DELICIOUS DRINK WOULD RESULT IF THE RED BERRIES OF THE COFFEE BUSH WERE ROASTED, GROUND AND INFUSED IN HOT WATER, HERE IS ONE OF THE LEGENDS, SAID TO BE FIRST TOLD IN 1670 OR THEREABOUTS BY A MARONITE SCHOLAR BY THE NAME OF ANTONIO FAUSTO NAIRONE.

AN ARABIAN GOATHERD noticed that his goats remained frisky all night when they'd eaten the leaves and berries of a certain shrub. He reported this to the imam of the local mosque. The imam took some branches of the shrub back to the mosque and ate one of the berries. It was bitter and unpleasant. He crushed some of the berries and boiled them, but the result was not good.

Next he decided to try roasting them. The aroma was exquisite; encouraged he crushed the berries and added a little hot water. It was a bitter brew so he stirred in some honey and was pleased with the taste. A few minutes later his heart started to beat faster and he found that hours later he was still wide awake. When he gave his decoction to some others in the mosque, the same thing happened to them. And that's how coffee was invented.

A cautionary note: the French novelist Honoré de Balzac (1799-1850)

drank 50 cups of coffee a day and died of caffeine poisoning.

AULUS VITELLIUS (15-69 AD), was briefly the Emperor of

Rome. He was a noted glutton and would often

accept dinner invitations to six different houses on the

same day. He would visit each house in turn and eat

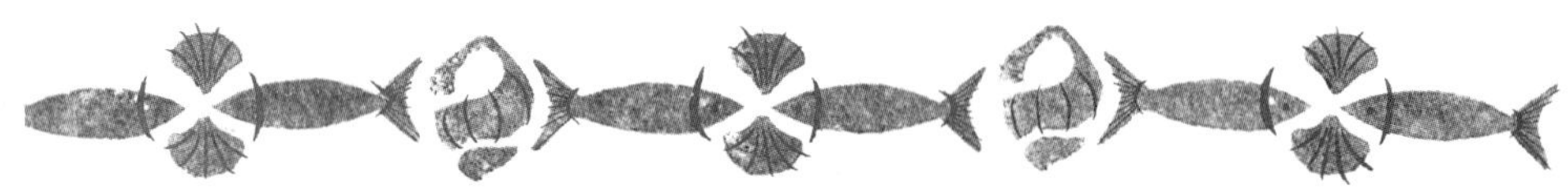

all the food that was offered. He is said to have

attended sacrifices and, not being able to hold himself

back, devoured the roasting sacrificial animals in the

middle of the ceremony!

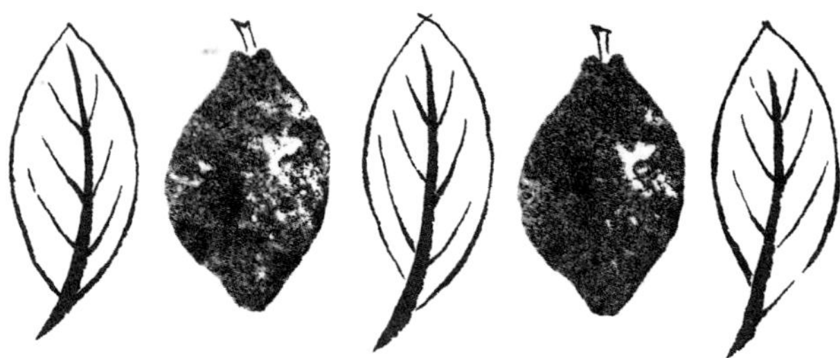

A FRENCH POLITICAL ÉMIGRÉ D'ALBIGNAC, is credited with introducing real (as opposed to 'boiled') salad dressings to England. He fled to London during the French Revolution where, after showing some fashionable young men in a tavern how a salad should be made, he hit on the idea of earning his living by making salads for the wealthy. At mealtimes he drove around London in his open carriage, calling at the various households where he had been summoned, and making their salads. A servant carried a mahogany case containing all the ingredients needed for d'Albignac's dressings: oils, vinegars, caviar, truffles, anchovies. He became known as 'the fashionable salad-maker' and was so successful that he had salad dressing cases made up which he stocked himself and sold by the hundred.

Most stories about how particular dishes were invented and named come to us through oral history and have, no doubt, been embellished over time. Here is the story of how *Épigrammes of Lamb* came into existence. In the eighteenth century, gastronomical snobbery was on the rise and it was the business of the lady of the house to make sure her chef's creations outshone those of her peers. One day a French lady had guests for dinner and she overheard one of them say that he had enjoyed excellent epigrams the night before at a nobleman's house. Thinking that her guest was referring to a new dish, the lady told her chef that he must prepare epigrams for the following day. He could find no recipe for such a dish, so he made it up: breast of lamb, poached, pressed and cut into heart shapes, and lamb cutlets, both coated in breadcrumbs and grilled.

TOMATOES WERE BROUGHT TO SPAIN FROM PERU at the end of the sixteenth century. Italy seems to have been the first European country, after Spain, to use them in any quantity. There is evidence that Italians were cooking with tomatoes in the seventeenth century, but they didn't appear in English cookbooks until the beginning of the nineteenth century. In the intervening 200 years, tomatoes (or golden apples, or love apples as they were called) were regarded with suspicion. It was felt that they were merely ornamental shrubs and that eating the fruit caused gout and cancer. They were also rumoured to excite the sexual appetite (hence love apples) — perhaps an additional reason to avoid them. Even in France the tomato was slow to catch on. In 1803 the gourmand Brillat-Savarin wrote, 'This vegetable or fruit, as one may call it, was almost wholly unknown in Paris 15 years ago.'

In the United States tomatoes were grown for consumption as early as 1806, but people were wary of eating them raw. One brave man, Colonel Robert Gibbon Johnson, publicly ate a raw tomato in 1840 to prove it was safe, but in 1860 in *Goday's Lady's Book*, housewives were still being urged to cook tomatoes for no less than three hours.

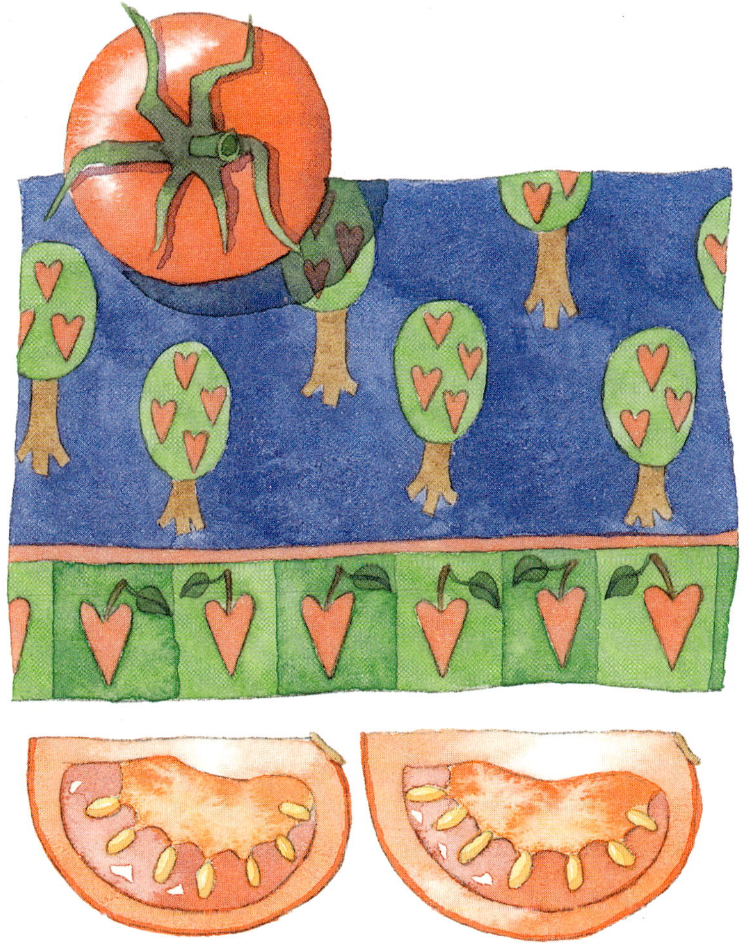

ONSIDERING HOW POPULAR POTATOES ARE today, their road to acceptance was long and hard. Antoine-Auguste Parmentier (whose name now graces several potato dishes), an army pharmacist, was a prisoner of war in Prussia when he first tasted potatoes. On returning to France in 1763 he urged his countrymen to taste this new vegetable which had come to Europe from the Americas. Convinced that you could develop leprosy from eating potatoes, the French refused to grow them.

King Louis XVI even tried the ruse of growing potatoes under heavy guard to make them seem precious. At night the guard was deliberately relaxed so that thieves could creep into the royal garden and steal the potatoes. But even then the eating of potatoes was not widespread — people simply didn't know what to do with them — some even ate them raw and unpeeled, and pronounced them disgusting. It wasn't until the Revolution that potatoes began to be eaten regularly in France — and that was because the people were so hungry that they had to make a virtue of necessity.

POTATOES WERE INTRODUCED TO IRELAND in the late sixteenth century and were a staple food until the potato famine of 1845. They were not as popular in England — probably because they were thought of as food for the poor and country people had to be paid premiums to grow them. Potatoes seemed to have gained currency by 1733 when Stephen Switzer, a garden designer and seedsman to the aristocracy, described the potato as 'That which was heretofore reckon'd a food fit only for Irishmen, and clowns, is now become the diet of the most luxuriously polite.' By 1840 baked potatoes were being sold in the streets of London, it was a thriving trade — with people from all classes buying them.

PORTABLE SOUP OR POCKET SOUP was the forerunner of our stock cubes. Made of beef or veal stock, much reduced and left to dry it could be cut into small pieces and carried in the pocket or little tin boxes. It was said to keep, when dry, for several years in any climate. When required, boiling water was added, and it was stirred until dissolved. Herbs and seasonings could be added as desired.

The French cookery writer, Menon, in his book, *La Cuisinière Bourgeoise*, published in 1746, mentioned that you could buy portable soup from a shop in the Boulevard St Germain. He recommended it for soldiers in the field. The English writer, Hannah Glasse has a recipe for Pocket Soup in her book, *The Art of Cookery, Made Plain and Easy*, published in 1758.

Watkin Tench, a captain-lieutenant of the First Fleet to Botany Bay, Australia writes about portable soup (or the lack of it) in his account of the 36 week journey. 'Of 212 marines we lost only one: and of 775 convicts put on board in England, but 24 perished in our route. To what cause are we to attribute this unhoped for success?

I wish I could answer to the liberal manner in which government supplied the expedition. But when the reader is told that some of the necessary articles allowed to ships on a common passage to the West Indies were withheld from us; that portable soup, wheat and pickled vegetables were not allowed, ... his surprise will redouble at the results of the voyage.'

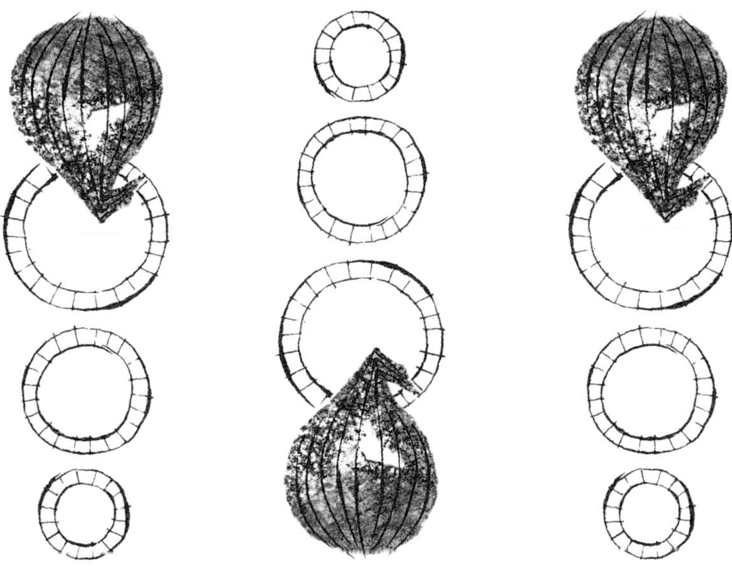

SOUFFLÉ POTATOES, LIKE MANY OTHER WONDERFUL DISHES, were discovered by accident. A banquet was planned for King Louis Philippe and Queen Amelie of France in 1837 to celebrate the opening of the first railway line between Paris and Saint-Germain. The King and Queen were to travel on the train, and a fairly simple meal had been planned for the royal couple, which included roast fillet of beef and fried potatoes. The chef began to cook the potatoes but was informed that the train was running late, so he took them out of the pan before they were completely cooked. They looked pale and wrinkled, and he was a worried chef when he put them back into very hot oil just before serving time. They puffed up like balloons and turned a delicious golden brown. The King was impressed and soufflé potatoes were born.

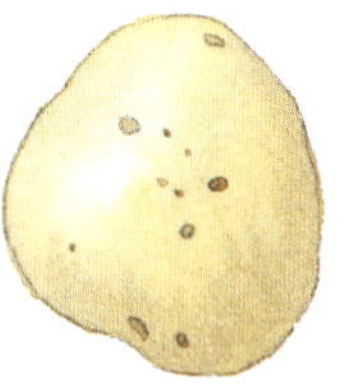   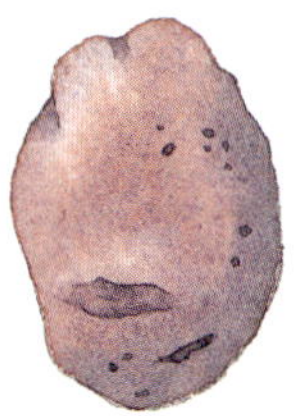

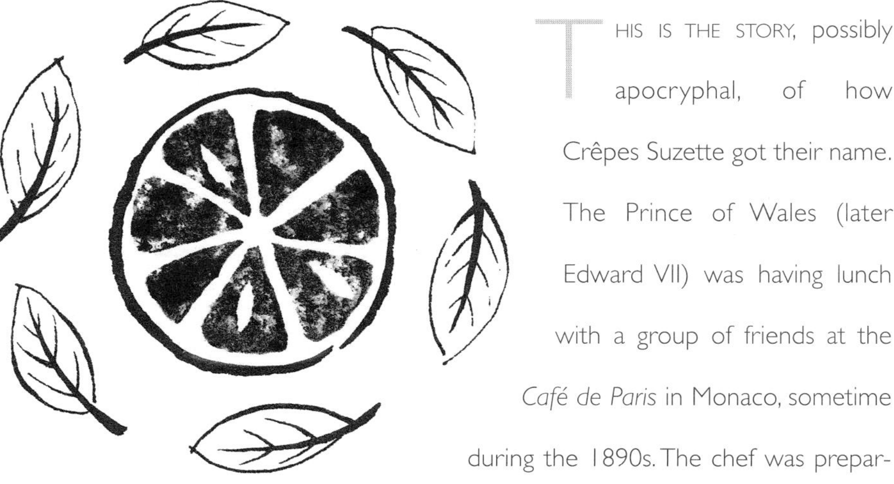

THIS IS THE STORY, possibly apocryphal, of how Crêpes Suzette got their name. The Prince of Wales (later Edward VII) was having lunch with a group of friends at the *Café de Paris* in Monaco, sometime during the 1890s. The chef was preparing crêpes in an orange sauce in a pan beside the Prince's table. The pan accidentally caught fire, but when the chef tasted the sauce it was so delicious that he added some more liqueur and this time deliberately lit it.

Delighted with the dish, the Prince asked its name. The chef wanted to name it after the Prince, but since most dessert dishes had a feminine name, and there was a young woman called Suzette in the party, the dish was named after her.

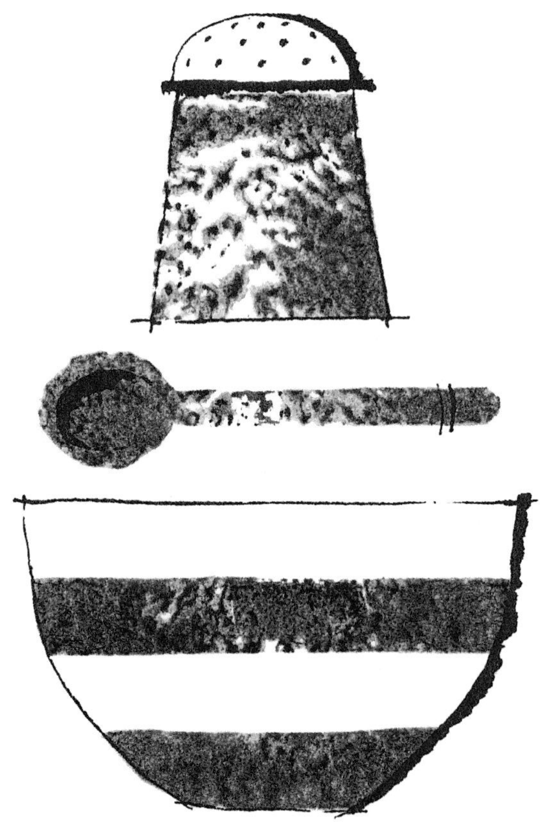

WHEN FINE WHEAT FLOUR WAS MADE UNIVERSALLY AVAILABLE in America in the first half of the nineteenth century, cake-making in the home became very popular. Charles Latrobe, who toured America in the early 1830s, wrote about the ubiquitous cake in his book, *The Rambler in North America* (1835).

> *'Nowhere is the stomach of the traveller or visitor put in such constant peril as among the cake-inventive housewives and daughters of New England. Such is the universal attention paid to this particular branch of epicurism in these states that I greatly suspect that some of the Pilgrim fathers must have come over to the country with the Cookery book under one arm and the Bible under the other.'*

Notwithstanding this seeming embarrassment of cakes, they were not easy to make, and required great physical stamina. One contemporary recipe calls for eggs and sugar to be beaten together for three-quarters of an hour!

FRANCES TROLLOPE (1780-1863), mother of novelist Anthony Trollope lived for a time in America and wrote a book about her experiences there: *Domestic Manners of the Americans*, published in 1832. Her stay in America was not a success, she considered herself superior to the natives and let them know exactly where they had gone wrong. 'In eating, they mix things together with the strangest incongruity imaginable. I have seen eggs and oysters eaten together; the sempiternal ham with apple-sauce... and salt fish with onions. The bread is everywhere excellent, but they rarely enjoy it themselves, as they insist upon eating horrible half-baked hot rolls both morning and evening.'

And on the eating of watermelon: 'Many wagon-loads of enormous water-melons were brought to market every day, and I was sure to see groups of men, women, and children seated on the pavement... sucking in prodigious quantities of this water fruit. Their manner of devouring them is extremely unpleasant; the huge fruit is cut into half a dozen sections, of about a foot long, and then, dripping as it is with water, applied to the mouth, from either side of which pour copious streams of the fluid, while, ever and anon, a mouthful of the hard black seeds are shot out in all directions, to the great annoyance of all within reach.'

FAMOUS FOOD LOVERS

THE FIRST COOKBOOK THAT WE KNOW ABOUT is said to have been written by the Roman gourmet, Apicius, in the first century AD. The book was compiled three centuries after Apicius's death, and since there were three men named Apicius who might have been the author, its origins are unclear.

The book gives us a glimpse of the food eaten by the ancient Roman upper classes. Romans didn't sit down to eat, they reclined on couches. They propped themselves up with their left forearms and stretched out to the table to take their food and wine in their right hands. They wore special dining clothes — a tunic and shawl — which were never to be worn out of doors. Each diner had two napkins, one tied around his neck and one to wipe his fingers. These would seem to be absolutely necessary as it can't have been easy to eat neatly while lying down. Forks were not known then — their only implements were knives and spoons, and food was picked up with the fingers. Apicius's recipes show that the food was by no means dry so the dishes must have been difficult and messy to eat.

The food that Apicius describes is heavily seasoned with herbs and spices and nearly all the recipes contain garum, a pungent fish sauce. It appears that many of the dishes, no matter what their main ingredient, would have tasted the same. Fish was a favourite food, followed by suckling pig and hare. Thrushes were the most prized birds, but they also ate grouse, partridge, guinea fowl, chicken, duck, ostrich, flamingo, parrot and crane. There was a gap of 13 centuries between Apicius's book and the next known cookbook.

HERE IS APICIUS'S RECIPE FOR STUFFED DORMICE — A ROMAN DELICACY.

'Stuff the dormice with minced pork, the minced meat of whole dormice, pounded with pepper, pine kernels, asafoetida, and liquamen [garum]. Sew up, place on a tile, put in the oven.'

THE FIRST ENGLISH COOKBOOK was published in 1500. Called *This is the Boke of Cokery*, it was meant for noble families and contained instructions for 'festes royalle'. Later in the sixteenth century and in the seventeenth century, more modest cookbooks were produced, aimed at the 'Hus-Wife', one of which boasted of 'contayning the inward and outward vertues which ought to be in a compleat woman'.

All the books recommended plain, 'English' cooking and condemned the wasteful French. Hannah Glasse was probably the most influential cookery writer in eighteenth century England. Her book, *The Art of Cookery Made Plain and Easy*, was published in 1747 and was very successful. It was written for servants and cooks of the gentry.

> *'I have taken upon me to instruct them [servants] in the best manner I am capable; and I dare say, that every Servant who can but read will be capable of making a tolerable good Cook, and those who have the least Notion of Cookery can't miss of being very good ones. If I have not wrote in the high, polite Stile, I hope I shall be forgiven; for my Intention is to instruct the lower Sort, and therefore must treat them in their own Way.'*

She railed strongly against French extravagance in cooking, and urged her English reader to cook plain, simple food. 'If Gentlemen will have French Cooks, they must pay for French tricks... I have heard of a Cook that used six Pounds of Butter to fry twelve Eggs, when every Body knows, that understands Cooking, that Half a Pound is full enough, or more than need be used: But then it would not be French.'

N THE SEVENTEENTH CENTURY Hannah Wolley wrote a book called *The Compleat Servantmaid; or the Young Maiden's Tutor* in which she spelt out the proper terms to be used when carving. As well as providing some colourful expressions, it gives us an idea of the range of foods that were eaten at the time. Beef and mutton were presumably simply 'carved'.

'thigh that Woodcock, thigh that Pigeon ... mince that Plover, wing that Quail, and wing that Partridge, allay that Pheasant, untack that Curlew, unjoint that Bittern, disfigure that Peacock, display that Crane, dismember that Heron, unbrace that Mallard, frust that Chicken, spoil that Hen, sawce that Capon, lift that Swan, reer that Goose, tire that Egg: as to the flesh of Beasts, unlace that Coney, break that Deer, leach that Brawn: for Fish, chine that Salmon, string that Lamprey, splat that Pike, sawce that Plaice, and sawce that Tench, splay that Bream; side that Haddock, tush that Barbel, culpon that Trout, transom that Eel, tranch that Sturgeon, tame that Crab, barb that Lobster.'

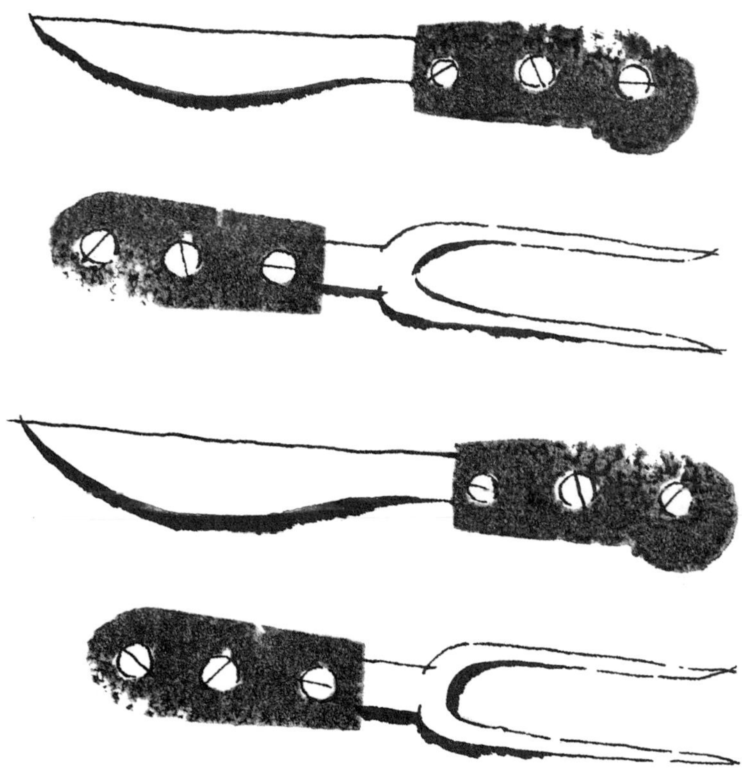

MME DE SÉVIGNÉ (1626-96), best known for the letters she wrote to her daughter about court life during the reign of Louis XIV, tells the sad tale of Vatel, steward to the Prince de Condé at Chantilly. When during a visit by the King, Vatel's expected supply of fish didn't turn up one morning, he became distraught and, declaring that 'I shall never survive this disgrace, my honour and my reputation are at stake', went to his room and ran a sword through his heart. 'Meanwhile', says Mme de Sévigné, 'the fish was coming in from all quarters'.

Many subsequent accounts present Vatel as a master chef. But the authors of *Larousse Gastronomique* are adamant that he was not a cook: 'his sensational suicide... shows that he did not have the character of a cook, because he did not know how to make the best of a bad job, could not rise above difficult circumstances.'

Hannah Glasse tells in *The Art of Cookery Made Plain and Easy*, how to raise a 'sallat' in two hours.

'Take fresh Horse-Dung hot, and lay it in a Tub near the Fire, then sprinkle some Mustard-seeds thick on it, and lay a thin Lay of Horse-Dung over it, cover it close and keep it by the Fire, and it will rise high enough to cut in two Hours.'

ANTONIN CARÊME (1784-1833) is the founder of classic French cooking. He has been called 'the cook of kings and the king of cooks'. While his dishes appear extravagant and ludicrously ornamental to modern tastes, it was Carême's passion for food, its quality and freshness, as well as its presentation, that made him such a great chef. Carême was born Marie-Antoine Carême of a poor family, one of 25 children. When he was twelve years old his father abandoned him in Paris and told him to use his wits to make his living.

The proprietor of a humble cookshop took him in and gave the young Carême his first lessons in cookery. At 15 he worked as a kitchen help in a restaurant and from there went to a fashionable *pâtissier*, M. Bailly, who impressed by Carême's talents, encouraged him in his passion for decorative 'set-pieces' of confectionery. Carême associated confectionery with architecture and his pastry and sugar constructions were based on engravings of buildings from old books that he pored over for hours.

He took copious notes about everything he cooked which he later used as material for his cookbooks. Carême worked for many famous men including the French diplomat Talleyrand, the Prince Regent (later George IV) of England, Czar Alexander I of Russia, the British Embassy in Paris and the Baron de Rothschild.

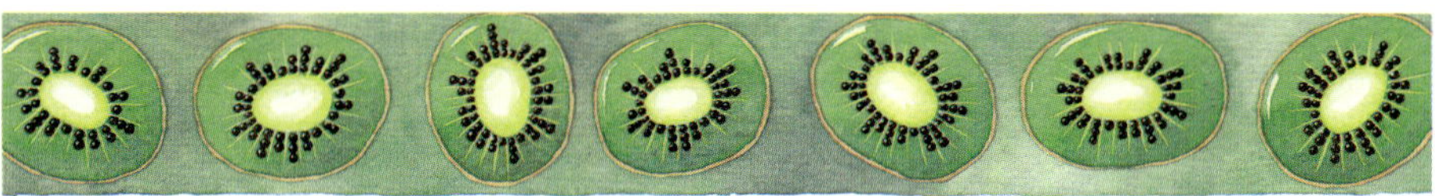

T SHOULDN'T BE THOUGHt that Carême's reputation rests solely on his elaborate presentations, although nowadays that's what most people associate with him. Carême's food was extravagant and costly, he used dozens of different sauces and needed a huge well-staffed and well-equipped kitchen to produce his special dinners — but he had learned the art of cooking well.

He used fresh seasonal ingredients and his dishes, though complicated to make, had a truly wonderful flavour. Lady Morgan was a guest at a dinner held by M. and Mme

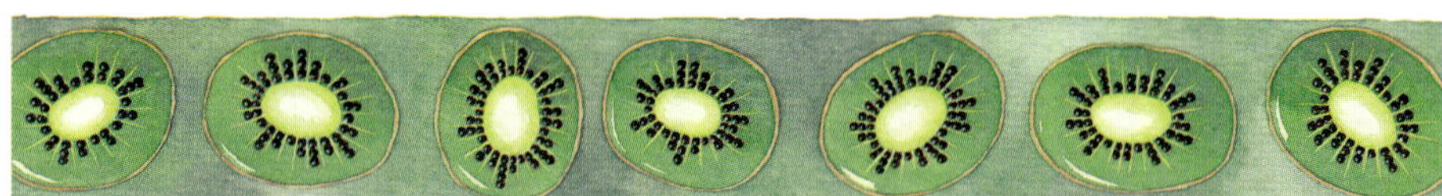

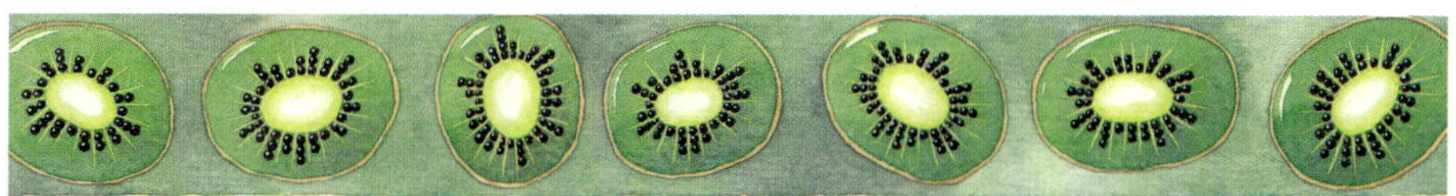

de Rothschild when Carême was presiding over the kitchen. 'The table arrangement and the dinner, everything, revealed Carême's hand. It was his brilliant variety, his perfect sense of proportion. No more English spices, no more black gravy: on the contrary, delicate flavours and the perfume of truffles... I state categorically that it has taken less genius to compose certain dramas than to execute this beautiful and elegant dinner.' Carême wrote numerous cookbooks, some of which he illustrated himself, and two books on architecture. He died at 49, no doubt due in part to the amount of carbon monoxide he breathed in from the coal fires in the badly ventilated kitchens in which he worked.

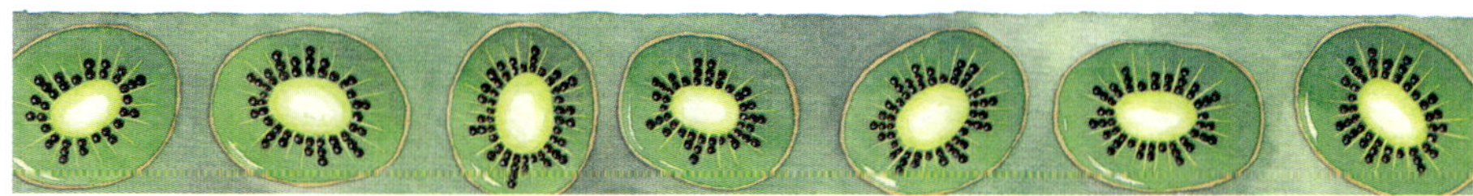

COOKBOOK AUTHOR ELIZA ACTON is not nearly as well known as the woman who followed her 15 years later, Isabella Beeton. Yet most contemporary cookery writers believe that Eliza Acton's book, *Modern Cookery for Private Families*, published in 1845, was far better than Mrs Beeton's *Book of Household Management* and that Mrs Beeton plagiarised Miss Acton to a considerable extent.

The story goes that Eliza Acton approached a publisher with the view to writing poetry. The publisher told her that books of poetry written by maiden ladies didn't sell and advised her to write a cookbook instead. *Modern Cookery* was the first English cookbook to give explicit instructions to the cook — both in the quantity of ingredients and in the method of cooking. This form of recipe writing was followed by Mrs Beeton and has continued to the present day.

Eliza Acton's book was not as resolutely English as earlier cookbooks; nevertheless only 15 out of 650 pages were devoted to 'foreign' food. Her book has been reissued and many of her dishes are still used today, without modification.

M RS BEETON IS PROBABLY THE MOST FAMOUS COOKERY WRITER of all time, certainly in the English language. She has become an embodiment of cookery. 'You're a regular Mrs Beeton' people say, when a recipe turns out well. Recipes appear in cookbooks with names such as Mrs Beeton's mincemeat, or Mrs Beeton's steak and kidney pudding, and everyone knows that it will be a good recipe: wholesome and reliable.

Isabella Beeton was not formally trained in cooking (except for some classes that she took in pastry-making), although as a young unmarried woman she no doubt learned a lot while helping her mother to bring up 20 younger brothers and sisters. At the age of 20 she married the publisher, Samuel Beeton and began writing for his *The Englishwoman's Domestic Magazine*. She contributed articles on food and household management, etiquette and fashion.

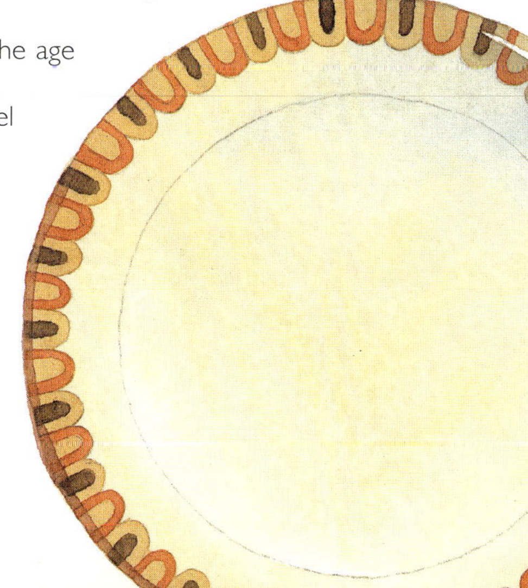

SABELLA BEETON's *Book of Household Management* was published in 1861 when she was 25. It had originally appeared in three parts during 1859-60. It was directed towards middle-class Victorian families and, as well as recipes, it contained instructions for the management of servants, list of foods in season and information about all aspects of running a house.

Many of the recipes in the book had been sent to her by readers of *The Englishwoman's Domestic Magazine*. For example, hers was the first printed recipe for steak and kidney pudding — and she attributed the recipe to a reader in Sussex. All previous recipes for this dish were made with steak only, no kidney. *Household Management* was a success right from the start. It was very 'English' and had a common sense approach with recipes written in plain language. Isabella Beeton died at 29, a week after giving birth to her fourth child. Since her death, her book has gone through many editions — and many revisions. Recipes have been altered to accommodate different tastes, some have been deleted altogether and new ones added. But the book, and its spin-offs keep selling, all because of that magic name, Mrs Beeton.

A LTHOUGH BORN IN FRANCE, Georges Auguste Escoffier (1847-1935) spent over 30 years working in England. He took charge of the kitchens of the newly built Savoy Hotel in London in 1890, where he stayed for eight years before moving on to work at the Carlton Hotel in London where he remained until he retired at the age of 74. At the Carlton he revolutionised the way that professional kitchens were run. Formerly one person was responsible for each dish and if, for example, that dish required béchamel sauce, he would make it — even if at the same time in another part of the kitchen, a cook might be making a béchamel sauce for a different dish. Escoffier reorganised his kitchens so that there were sauce makers, pastry makers, soup makers and cooks who made only cold dishes. Once the new system was in place, it made for much faster and more efficient food preparation. Escoffier also banned the habit the chefs had got into of 'tippling' through the day.

The Carlton, like the other great hotels, welcomed women into its dining rooms and became a fashionable place to eat and to be seen. Late suppers after the theatre were popular and Sunday, when the household servants had their day off, was also a busy time for the hotel kitchens. Escoffier was under heavy pressure from his wealthy clientele to produce 'new' dishes. He wrote, 'Personally I have ceased counting the nights spent in the attempt to discover new combinations, when, completely broken with the fatigue of the heavy day, my body ought to have been at rest.'

Sometimes he would look back to the food of his native Provence for inspiration, but he hugely modified these essentially peasant dishes, replacing oil with butter, discarding garlic and adding truffles or other *haute cuisine* refinements. In 1920 the French President, Poincaré, presented Escoffier with the cross of the Chevalier of the Legion of Honour in recognition of the work he had done to promote and enhance the prestige of French cooking throughout the world.

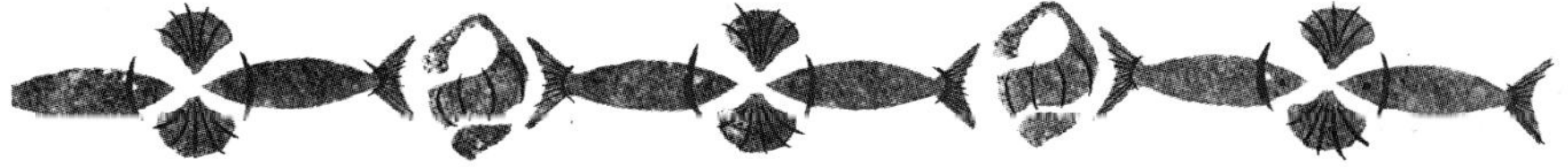

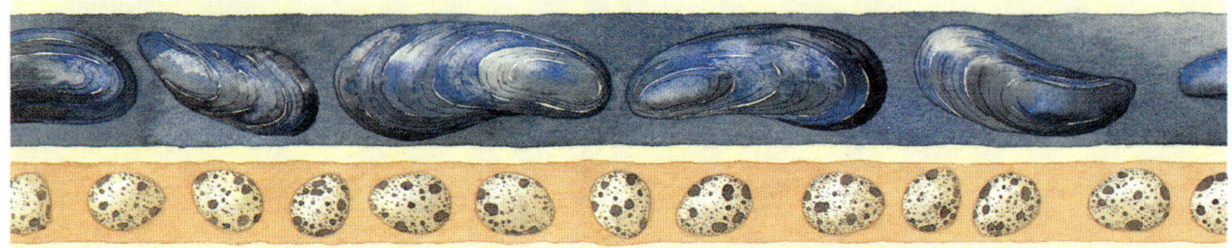

AUGUSTE ESCOFFIER WROTE SEVERAL COOKBOOKS, the most
famous of which, *Le Guide Culinaire*, published in 1903, is
still used today in cooking schools. In fact, a poor imitation of
Escoffier's style of cooking can still be seen in the dining rooms
of hotels around the world. Escoffier's style was *Le Grande*

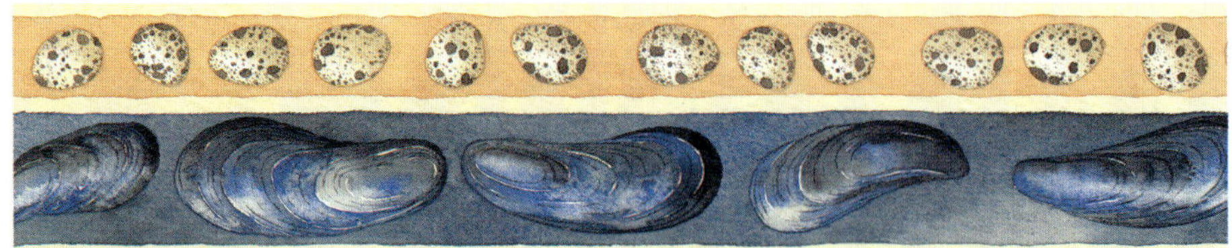

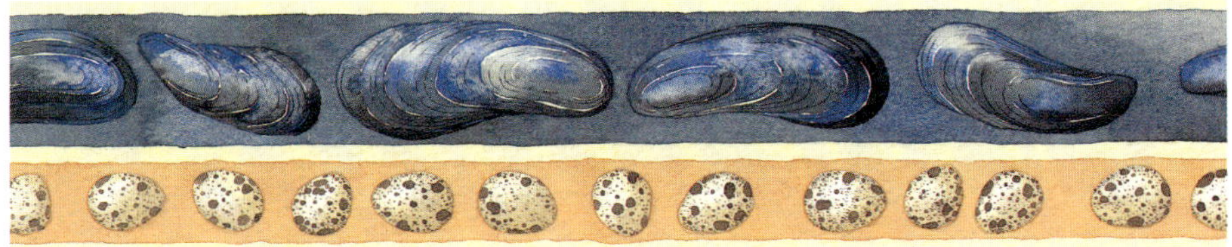

Cuisine, the same as Carême's, but over the years he modified his dishes, lightening and simplifying them. He even rejected the wax flowers and ornamental table decorations that he had used in his early days. An updated form of *Escoffier-cuisine* lasted until the 1960s and the birth of *Nouvelle Cuisine*.

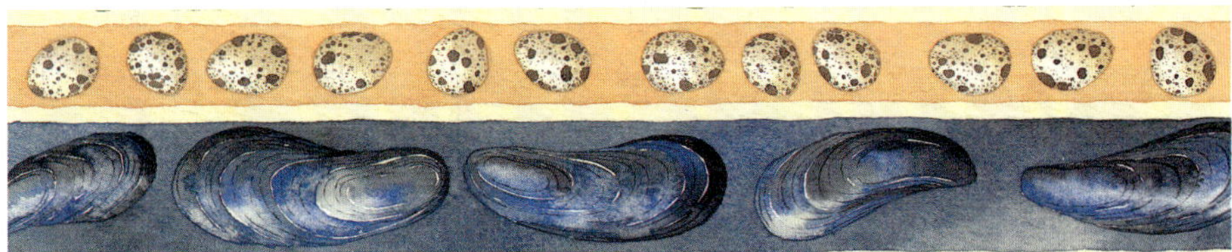

THE AMERICAN WRITER MFK FISHER (1908-1992) WRITES ABOUT FOOD IN SUCH A WAY THAT YOU FEEL IT IS THE MOST INTERESTING SUBJECT THAT ANYONE COULD WRITE ABOUT. THE MOST FAMOUS OF HER BOOKS, *THE ART OF EATING*, PUBLISHED IN 1954, IS AN OMNIBUS VOLUME CONTAINING FIVE OF HER EARLY WORKS.

SHE WEAVES HER LIFE STORY IN AND OUT OF ANECDOTES AND PHILOSOPHICAL DISCUSSIONS ABOUT FOOD AND SHE WRITES BEAUTIFULLY. HER EVOCATIVE ESSAYS — ON A SOLITARY LUNCH AT A FAMOUS FRENCH RESTAU-RANT WITH A FANATICAL WAITRESS, OR ON SHIPBOARD DINING IN THE LATE 1930s — ARE FUNNY AND POIGNANT. THE POET, W.H. AUDEN, ONCE SAID OF MFK FISHER, 'I DO NOT KNOW OF ANYONE IN THE UNITED STATES WHO WRITES BETTER PROSE'.

ELIZABETH DAVID (1913-1992) is responsible, more than any other contemporary cookery writer, for changing the way we eat and our attitude towards food. Her books are far from simple recipe books: she writes about the history of food, tells stories about the food she's eaten in various countries and stresses the importance of fresh seasonal produce. If you cook from Elizabeth David's books, two things will happen: first, every recipe will turn out perfectly — the timing is right, the quantities are right, and the taste is wonderful. Secondly, everyone who eats your food will think you're a marvellous cook. Thousands of 'good cooks' today owe their reputation to Elizabeth David.

BRILLAT-SAVARIN (1755-1826) WAS A FRENCH MAGISTRATE, politician and gastronome. He fled to the United States during the French Revolution, where, he says, he introduced Americans to scrambled eggs. On returning to France he eventually became a member of the French Court of Appeal.

However, what he is remembered for is his book, *The Physiology of Taste*. He had been keeping notes for 30 years on every aspect of taste, from its effect on the senses to manners at the table and he published the book himself in 1826, shortly before his death. One of the most widely praised translations was done by the American writer, MFK Fisher, who said she fell in love with him while she was working on it. Brillat-Savarin wasn't a cook himself, he was a food philosopher. He is best known for his aphorisms. Here are some of them.

• *A dessert course with no cheese is a beauty with only one eye.* •

• *[the turkey is] the best gift of the New World to the Old.* •

• *The world is nothing without life, and all that lives takes nourishment.* •

• *Animals feed: man eats: only the man of intellect knows how to eat.* •

• *The fate of nations depends on the way they eat.* •

• *Tell me what you eat: I will tell you what you are.* •

• *The Creator, who made man such that he must eat to live, incites him to eat by means of appetite, and rewards him with pleasure.* •

• *Gourmandism is an act of judgement, by which we give preference to things which are agreeable to our taste over those which are not.* •

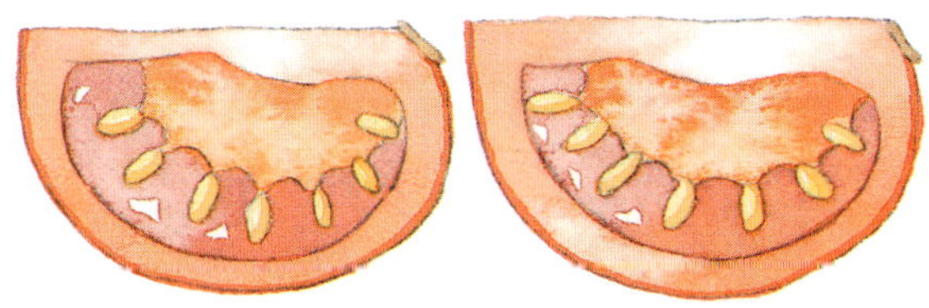

RILLAT-SAVARIN HAD A THEORY that you could tell a gourmand from their physiognomy. To be predestined to be a gourmand you should be of medium height, you should have a round or square face, bright eyes, a small forehead, a short nose, full lips and a well-rounded chin.

If you are a woman you should be buxom, pretty rather than beautiful and have a tendency to run to fat. Women who prefer sweet dishes above all others will have fine features, a delicate air, neat figures and 'above all, a very special way with their tongues'.

FRENCH PHILOSOPHER AND SCIENTIST Bernard de Fontenelle (1657-1757) had a passion for asparagus. He liked to eat it with an oil dressing. One day the Abbé Terrasson called on him unexpectedly and asked if he might stay for dinner. Fontenelle was not pleased — he would have to share his asparagus. Grudgingly he ordered his cook to serve the Abbé's half with white sauce, as was the Abbé's preference, and his own portion with oil dressing. Just before dinner the Abbé experienced some kind of seizure and fell down dead on the floor. Fontenelle rushed into the kitchen, shouting, 'All the asparagus with oil'.

SAMUEL JOHNSON (1709-1784), THE NOTED MAN OF LETTERS, immortalised by his friend James Boswell in Boswell's *Life of Johnson*, was quite a glutton.

'When at table, he was totally absorbed in the business of the moment;

his looks seemed rivetted to his plate; nor would he, unless when in very

high company, say one word, or even pay the least attention to what

was said by others, till he had satisfied his appetite, which was so fierce,

and indulged with such intenseness, that while in the act of eating, the

veins of his forehead swelled, and generally a strong perspiration was

visible. To those whose sensations were delicate, this could not but be dis-

gusting; and it was doubtless not very suitable to the character of a

philosopher, who should be distinguished by self command.'

Dr Johnson was, however, according to Boswell 'or affected to be, a man of very

nice discernment in the science of cookery.' And 'he was not pleased if something bet-

ter than a plain dinner was not prepared for him. I have heard him say on such

an occasion, "This was a good dinner enough, to be sure; but it was not a dinner

to ask a man to.'"

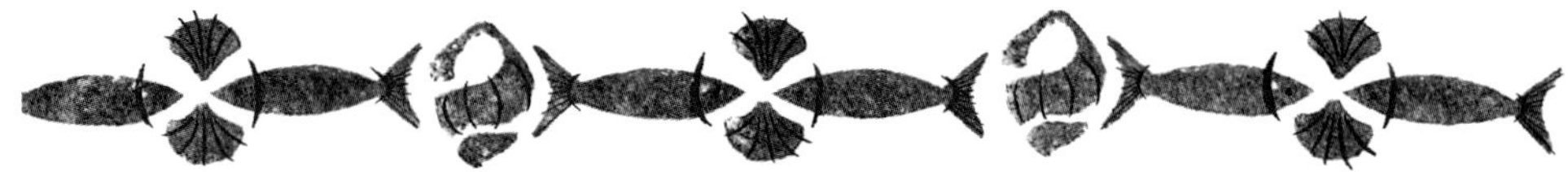

JAMES WOODFORDE, SUB-WARDEN AT NEW COLLEGE, Oxford, describes Christmas dinner for 15 guests in 1773. 'We had for dinner two fine cods boiled, with fried soles round them, and oyster sauce, a fine sirloin of beef roasted, some pease soup and an orange pudding, for the first course; for the second we had a lease of wild ducks roasted, a fore-quarter of lamb, and salad, and mince pies... After the second course there was a fine plum cake... We dined at three o'clock and were an hour and a half at it.'

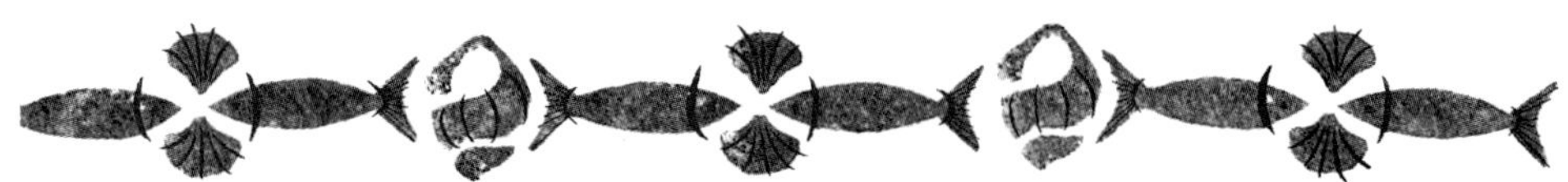

T HAS ALWAYS BEEN CONSIDERED unlucky for 13 to sit down to dinner.

So if 14 people are asked, and one drops out at the last minute, who can you call at such short notice to fill the gap? This problem was solved in nineteenth century Paris by a group of men who called themselves quatorzièmes (fourteenths). Every night between 5 and 9pm, they would sit at home suitably dressed, waiting for a summons to dinner. If they were sent for, they'd appear in the drawing room: experienced, charming, professional diners.

F ONE OF THE SIGNS of a gastronomic revolution is a profusion of cookbooks on the market, then the end of the twentieth century is surely such a time. Never before have there been so many books on food: scholarly books on the history and sociology of food; books by restaurateurs; books on the food of different cultures; on single ingredients or types of dishes.

There are serious collections and quirky ones; books with beautiful colour photographs of the food arranged with crystal and china; and there are modest volumes decorated with simple line drawings. At the end of the twentieth century, it seems that we are seriously obsessed with food.

CHAPTER FOUR

FOOD FASHIONS

THE ANCIENT ROMANS LOVED OLIVE OIL. They rubbed it over their bodies and were massaged with it to reduce tension and fatigue. Soaps were made from it, women rubbed perfumed olive oil into their hair and Julius Caesar demanded an annual payment of three million litres of olive oil from Numidia (present-day Algeria) as a tribute.

It has always been the favoured cooking oil of people who live in Mediterranean countries, and although it's only recently that Anglo-Saxon nations have taken to olive oil, we've done so with such gusto that oil producing countries are finding it hard to keep up with the demand. Countries such as Australia, which previously did not have an olive industry, have started to grow olives in an effort to meet growing demand.

THE POPULARITY OF OLIVE OIL started to grow when it was learnt that people who used it liberally in their cooking — Italians, Spanish, French — suffer less heart disease than those who used butter for cooking. But the reason it has stayed popular is because of its taste. Once you have used a good olive oil in frying or salad dressings, nothing else will do.

Smart restaurants offer good chewy-crusted bread with a jar of pale green olive oil and a little dish of sea salt instead of the usual bread and butter. Extra virgin olive oil is sold, not just in delicatessens but in supermarkets too, and its high price does not deter the true believers.

PATRICK LAMB, who was 'near 50 years Master-Cook to their late Majesties King Charles II, King James II, King William and Queen Mary, and to Her Present Majesty Queen Anne' wrote a cookbook called *Royal Cookery*, published in 1710. This is one of his menus, for the month of August.

FIRST COURSE

Westphalia Ham and Chickens

Bisque of Fish

Haunch of Venison roasted

Venison-pasty

Roasted Fowls aladobe

Umble Pyes

White Fricassees of Chickens

Roasted Turkeys larded

Almond Florentines

Alamonde Beef

SECOND COURSE

Dish of Pheasant and Partridges

Roasted Lobsters

Broil'd Pike

Creamed Tart

Rock of Snow and Sullebubs

Dish of Sweetbreads

Sallad-Magundy

MEDIEVAL AND RENAISSANCE BANQUETS were served *à la francaise*, with everything on the table at once, similar to our modern day buffet. There were usually two courses — the table would be cleared once and the next 'buffet' laid out. This tradition survived at official banquets until the end of the nineteenth century.

T HE PRECURSOR OF THE PRESENT WESTERN STYLE of eating separate courses, *service à la russe*, is said to have been introduced to France in the 1830s by the Russian Prince Kourakin. It took a while to catch on but by the end of the nineteenth century *service à la russe* was beginning to be seen at formal meals and banquets. It required more servants than service *à la francaise*; also more china and cutlery. But it did mean that everyone got to taste everything.

At dinners *à la francaise*, especially if there were a lot of guests, diners would often content themselves with eating the dishes closest to hand, for fear of appearing greedy if they asked for dishes to be passed along the table.

THOMAS JEFFERSON (1743-1826), third president of the United States, is credited with introducing French food to America. Jefferson was minister to France between 1784-89; he had never tasted French cooking before and was full of praise for it. On his return home he sent for his erstwhile French chef and was soon serving his guests some of the food that had so attracted him in France.

When he became president in 1801 his chef prepared meals that caused one guest to remark, 'never before had such dinners been given at the President's house...'. The French influence was limited to a small circle, however, and did not affect most Americans. It was not seen again until the nineteenth century when French chefs started to open restaurants in New York.

D ELMONICOS RESTAURANT opened in New York in 1832, introducing French cooking to Americans. Only a select few had been able to experience the cooking of Thomas Jefferson's French chef at the Whitehouse, but with the opening of Delmonicos and the establishment of the first great hotels with their French chefs, upper-class Americans could taste classic French cooking for the first time in their own country.

Cooking schools for ladies opened and 'cuisine' began to be taken seriously by hostesses around the country. By the 1920s, however, the popularity of French cooking was replaced by German, Dutch and particularly, Italian food.

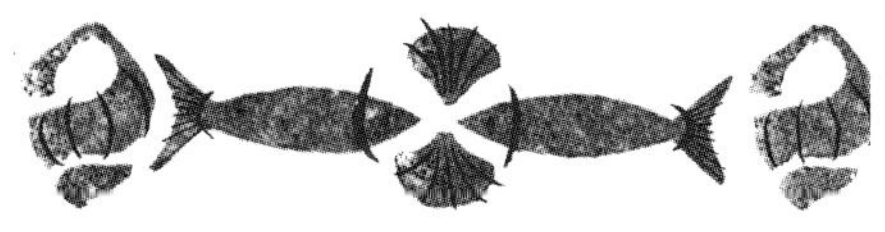

RANCOPHOBIA was never so plainly expressed as in the English distaste for French 'tricked-up' food and their own preference for 'Good Plain Cooking'. While there were famous French chefs presiding over the kitchens of the aristocracy and in some clubs and restaurants in the nineteenth century, middle-class families were disdainful of the French penchant for sauces, claiming that good meat did not need disguising.

The English thought that their produce, especially their meat, was superior to that grown in France and it needed no embellishment. One French cook went so far as to say, in 1813 that the English knew only one sauce: melted butter.

> *'Melted butter and anchovies, melted butter and capers, melted butter and parsley, melted butter and eggs, and melted butter forever...'*

J OINTS OF MEAT AND PIES were the order of the day in nineteenth-century England. Vegetables were relegated to a lowly position in the meal — they were boiled until soft and grey and served with the meat — rarely as a separate course. Vegetables were seldom mentioned on English menus — if they were, they were often called pot-herbs. The omission may be because they were rarely served or because they weren't thought important enough to mention. The French were criticised for eating so many vegetables and (comparatively) so little meat. Salads, if they appeared at all in an English meal, were limp, sodden affairs, often prepared and dressed an hour or so before the meal. Puddings, usually made with suet, were well loved and a dinner wasn't thought complete without a pudding or two.

THE UNITED STATES, 'GOOD PLAIN COOKING' was also considered the 'right' way to eat, influenced no doubt by the Puritan background of the English settlers and the no less strict simplicity of the Dutch and German immigrants.

But there was a much wider variety of vegetables in the New World. Harriet Beecher Stowe, author of *Uncle Tom's Cabin*, wrote about the abundance and variety of American vegetables in the 1860s.

> '... ripe juicy tomatoes, raw or cooked; cucumber in brittle slices; rich, yellow sweet potatoes; broad Lima beans, and beans of other and various names; tempting ears of Indian corn steaming in enormous piles, and great smoking tureens of the savoury succotash, an Indian gift to the table for which civilization need not blush; sliced egg plant in delicate fritters; and marrow squashes, of creamy pulp and sweetness: a rich variety, embarrassing to the appetite, and perplexing to the choice.'

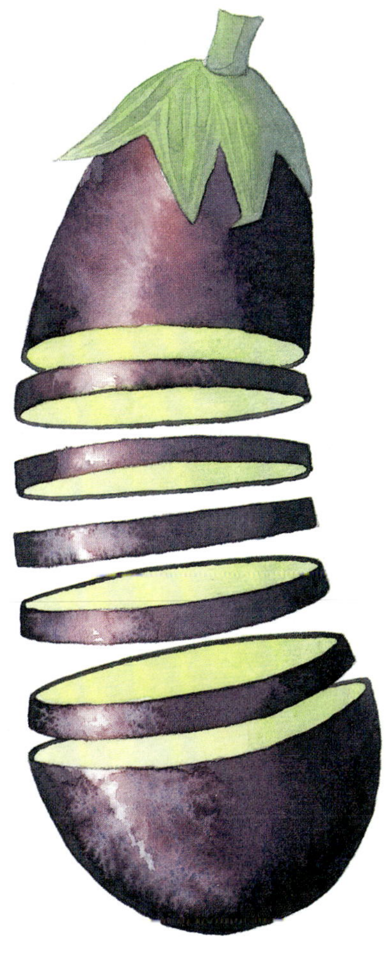

N 1905 A PENNSYLVANIA HOUSEWIFE won a national prize for a jellied salad. From then on, moulded food grew in popularity in the United States and was almost compulsory at smart luncheon and buffet parties in the 1920s and 30s. The brand name Jell-O, was given to flavoured gelatin by Pearl Wait, the wife of Paul Wait, a patent-medicine seller who had bought the rights to the gelatin powder in 1897.

A jellied salad was an ingenious way of serving raw vegetables. Instead of cutting them into strips and serving as *hors d'oeuvres*, picked up with the fingers and dipped into mayonnaise, they were suspended in a jelly, so the dish could be sliced and eaten with a fork with a spoonful of mayonnaise on the side, as a first course or an accompaniment to fish or poultry.

Some recipes were savoury and some were sweet, but a great number of them mixed sweet and savoury flavours together — often not very successfully. Finely diced raw vegetables were suspended in a lime-flavoured jelly; grated carrots were mixed with pecans and tinned pineapple and moulded in lemon-flavoured jelly. Seafood mousses became popular too, with crab, lobster and salmon predominating.

Gelatin desserts were promoted by gelatin manufacturers as 'dainty desserts for dainty people'. Although its popularity has waned over the past few decades, this American innovation, sometimes known as 'congealed salad', still has its followers in many parts of the United States, particularly in the south and west of the country.

S TARTED IN F RANCE DURING the 1960s, *Nouvelle Cuisine* reached its apotheosis in the mid-seventies with the publication of two books; *La Cuisine du marché* by Paul Bocuse and *La Grande Cuisine minceur* by Michel Guérard. Thanks mainly to these books it was taken up with enthusiasm in England and the United States. *Nouvelle Cuisine* was new because it moved away from the heavy flour-based sauces that had been so much a part of French food until then. It was lighter food, simpler, and less disguised. Thin sauces made from puréed vegetables or reductions of stock were spooned onto a plate (sometimes there were two sauces of different colours side by side on a big white plate) then the fillet of beef or lamb or the chicken breast or fish cutlet was placed on top of the sauce. It had a Japanese appearance — pure, with restrained garnishing.

Only ingredients that were in season were used; menus were short; steaming was employed much more than before; food was cooked for a shorter time and nutrition was taken into account when dishes were created. Practitioners used regional dishes, not *haute cuisine*, as the basis of the new food; they were inventive and daring and they used modern technology such as food processors and microwave ovens to help them. The most famous *Nouvelle Cuisine* chefs were Paul Bocuse, Michel Guérard, Jean and Pierre Troisgros and Roger Vergé.

A decline in *Nouvelle Cuisine* began during the late eighties. Although the food looked very pretty and tasted delicious, it was expensive and the portions were small. Diners started to long for warming, hearty dishes, and Comfort Food began to gain popularity. While *Nouvelle Cuisine* in its pure form did not last, it signalled the end of classic French cooking or *Grande Cuisine*, and paved the way for World Food — where several different cultural influences may appear in the same dish.

THE NUMBER OF PEOPLE who are vegetarians or semi-vegetarians (people who eat fish and white meat) is increasing. There are a number of reasons for this, the two main ones being religious beliefs and perceived health benefits.

But probably the major cause for the shift away from meat has been our increased knowledge of how animals are raised and slaughtered. You only have to read a description of the life of a battery hen to decide you really don't want to be part of that particular food chain. Many people can't eat veal because of the thought of how the young calf is reared; and after the recent film, *Babe*, thousands of people around the world swore off pork. Added to that Westerners, particularly Americans, are becoming more squeamish about cuts of meat that look like the animal they came from.

Fillets of chicken breast, pale innocuous shapes, are easier to cope with than a whole bird with its legs and wings. People are veering towards blander tastes in food too. In the United States and France, for example, game is eaten fresh — the idea of eating 'hung' game is not appealing.

IN THE UNITED STATES young, fit, health-conscious people rate salads as their favourite meal. The same is probably not true in Europe, but in warmer countries such as Australia, Californian-style salads with nuts and fruit and Asian salads with oriental vegetables, noodles and dressing, are gaining in popularity. In recent years mixed salad leaves or mesclun have become popular. Mesclun is usually a mixture of rocket (arugula), radicchio, baby spinach, lamb's lettuce (corn salad) and sometimes herb mixtures.

Another new development in salads is the introduction of hydroponically-grown lettuces which are bought still growing, with their roots enclosed in a little plastic bucket. Americans generally eat their salad first, before the main part of the meal begins. The French eat theirs after the main course. English and Australian diners usually eat their salad as an accompaniment to the main course.

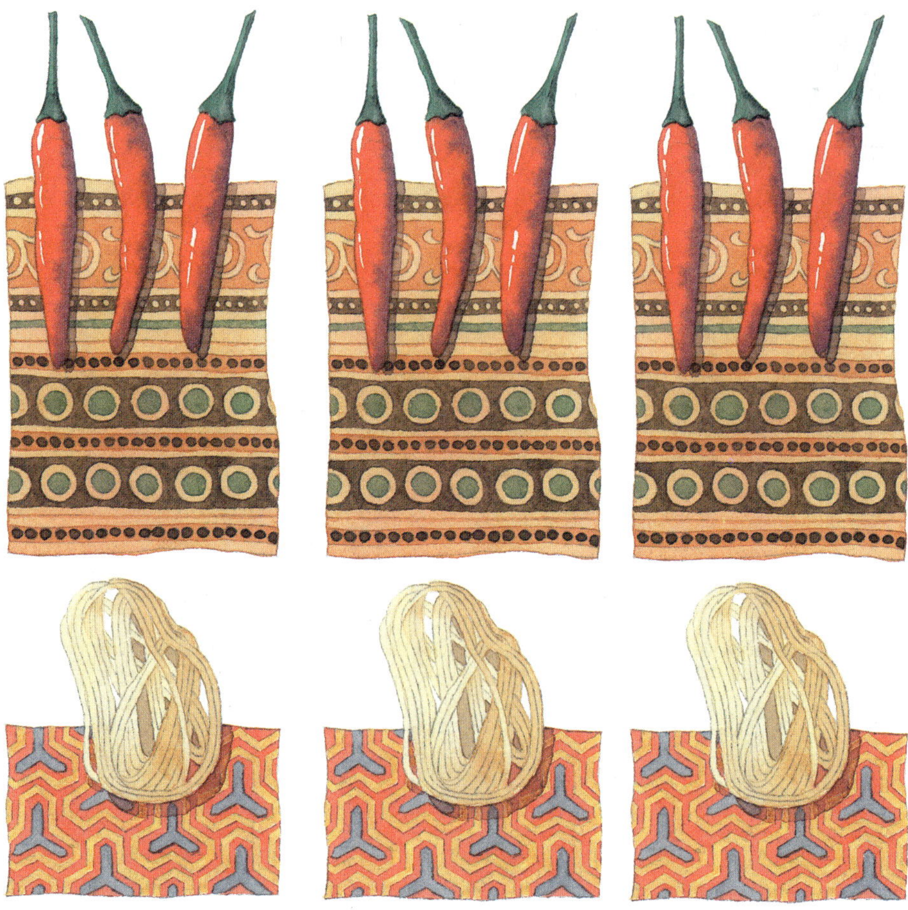

ORLD FOOD REFERS TO THOSE RESTAURANTS AND CAFÉS that include on their menus food from many different countries. Sydney, Australia is a particularly good example of how World Food has come to dominate the café scene. Asian food, especially Thai, is very popular in Sydney. There's usually at least one Thai dish on every café menu. American salads, especially Caesar salad can be found, along with hamburgers; Italian focaccias, toasted sandwiches made with Turkish bread and Mexican nachos will often be there. And, of course, there will always be a pasta dish or two.

Ingredients from different countries are often mixed in World Food. Lemongrass, galangal and chillies are found in dishes that would once have been called Mediterranean; dishes that could never be described as Chinese are stir-fried and crispy noodles are sprinkled over Californian salads. This kind of food is often called Pacific Rim. Purists say that it doesn't work, but in the hands of a sensitive, imaginative cook, it can be superb.

THE 1990s IS THE DECADE OF LOW-FAT FOOD. There's low-fat milk, cream, cheese, ice cream and salad dressing, and a huge number of other processed low-fat foods and drinks. Animals are specially bred with more muscle and less fat. When the meat is butchered, any fat that is there, is cut off. Pork is advertised as being as lean as beef, and beef is sold unmarbled; lamb is marketed as 'trim lamb', to distance it from

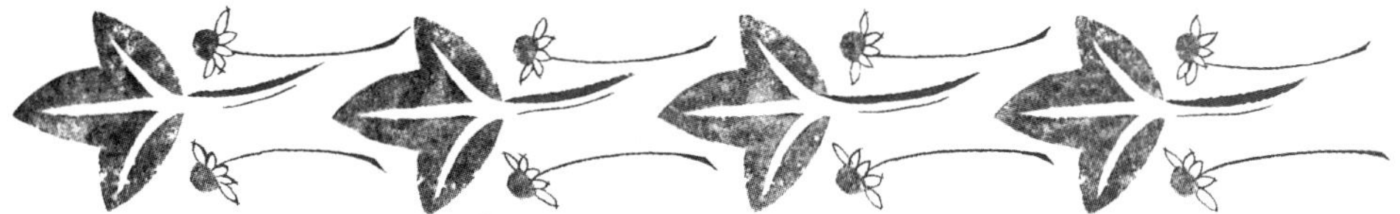

the old style of lamb which was perceived as fatty. Airlines cater for low-fat diets, skim milk cappuccino is served by all but the most adamantly purist Italian cafés.

Even fast food outlets are advertising low-fat hamburgers and fried chicken. In sandwich shops you're asked, 'would you like butter?' when a few years ago the bread would have been buttered long before lunch-time.

Comfort Food or Nursery Food has been on the fringes of fashion for the past 20 years. It's really nostalgia food. Unless the food you had as a child was execrable, from time to time you'll want to taste it again, particularly when you're tired or stressed.

Depending on your cultural background, you might crave apple pie, steamed pudding with custard, lamb chops, liver and bacon, hot cornbread, or simply a slice of bread and butter with a cup of tea. Nowadays you will find tripe and onions, corned (salt) beef with parsley sauce, brawn (headcheese), bread and butter pudding and bread pudding on some very smart menus.

Food pundits are predicting

that rice will be the

Next Big Thing.

CHAPTER FIVE

FOOD FACTS

THE EXPRESSION, 'TO SIT ABOVE THE SALT', means to sit in a place of distinction. At medieval banquets, special guests sat with the host at a raised 'high table' in the middle of which was placed the family's massive silver salt cellar. So the host and important guests sat 'above the salt' and less important guests sat 'below the salt'. The further away from the salt you sat, the lower your status.

AT A FORMAL DINNER IN FRANCE, THE FEMALE GUEST OF HONOUR SHOULD ALWAYS ACCEPT AN OFFER OF A SECOND HELPING BECAUSE ONLY IF SHE DOES CAN ANYONE ELSE HAVE ONE.

At a Chinese meal it is considered impolite to leave even one grain of rice

uneaten in your bowl.

BEDROOM SPICES WERE A MEDIEVAL TRADITION. THEY WERE WHOLE SEEDS OF CORIANDER, FENNEL AND ANISEED, EATEN RAW OR SOMETIMES COOKED IN SUGAR. PEOPLE OFTEN MET TO TALK IN BEDROOMS BECAUSE THE ROOMS WERE MORE COMFORT-ABLE AND PRIVATE THAN THE (WITH) DRAWING ROOMS. A LITTLE BOX OF SPICES WOULD BE HANDED AROUND, USUALLY AFTER THE WINE, TO SWEETEN THE BREATH.

The main meal of the day, dinner, was served at 11am in England at the beginning of the sixteenth century. It moved backward, hour by hour, until, by the end of the eighteenth century the main meal of the day, still called dinner, was eaten by the gentry at 7 or 8pm. Country folk and the working classes still ate their dinner early — at about 3pm.

I N EUROPE HOW YOU PLACE YOUR KNIFE AND FORK to indicate that you've finished eating differs widely. In Greece you cross your knife and fork on the plate, knife under the fork; fork with the tines down. In Belgium you place your knife and fork together across the top of the plate, pointing left; fork with the tines up. In France and Italy, knives and forks are placed together on the plate with the tines of the fork down. In England and most of the countries that started as English colonies, knives and forks are placed together

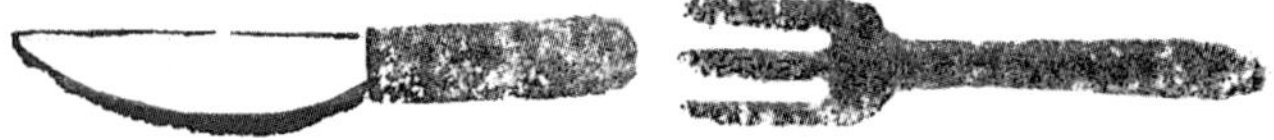

with the blade of the knife facing inwards and the tines of the fork up. In France diners are often supplied with knife and fork rests, so the same cutlery can be used for more than one course.

During the eighteenth and nineteenth centuries this custom applied in England and the United States — and perhaps in Canada too, if the much-told tale of the Canadian waitress and the member of the British royal family is true. 'Keep your fork, Duke,' she said, 'there's pie'.

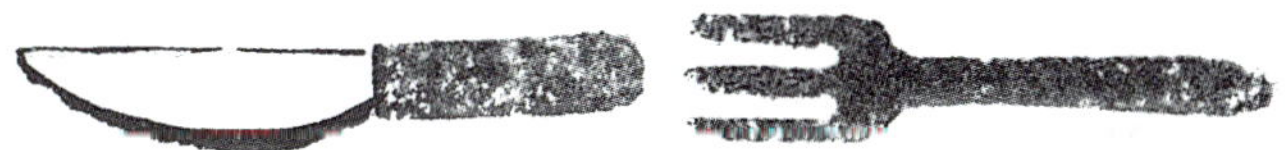

No more than five people may participate in a Japanese tea ceremony. A special tea, matcha, is used. It is emerald green and slightly bitter and is prepared by whipping it into hot water. Traditionally only one cup is made at first (in an exquisite cup) and each guest sips two or three times from it and, after carefully wiping the edge, passes it on to the next guest.

Sweetmeats are served and more tea is poured, this time in individual small cups. The four objectives of the tea ceremony are: to calm rough manners; to master the passions; to overcome antagonism and to establish peace.

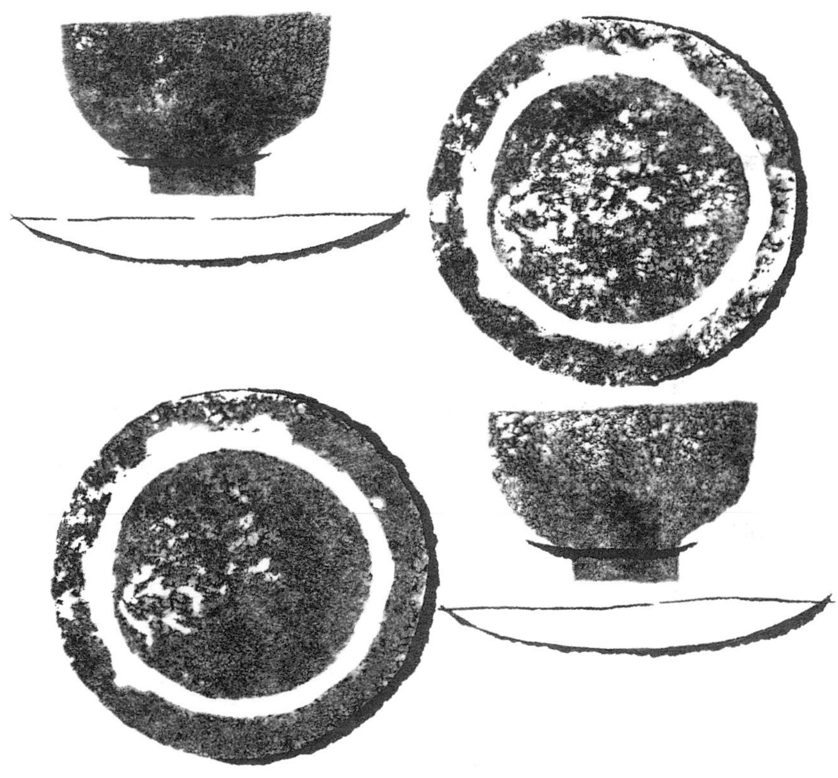

N JAPAN, DINERS PAY LARGE SUMS OF MONEY to eat fugu (puffer fish or blowfish). The intestines, ovaries, skin and liver contain a potent toxin — a tiny sliver is enough to kill you. Fugu chefs must undergo a seven-year apprenticeship to learn how to remove the poisonous parts. Despite this, dozens of people die from fugu poisoning every year.

The eating of fugu has been described as being like playing a game of Russian roulette, which seems to be its

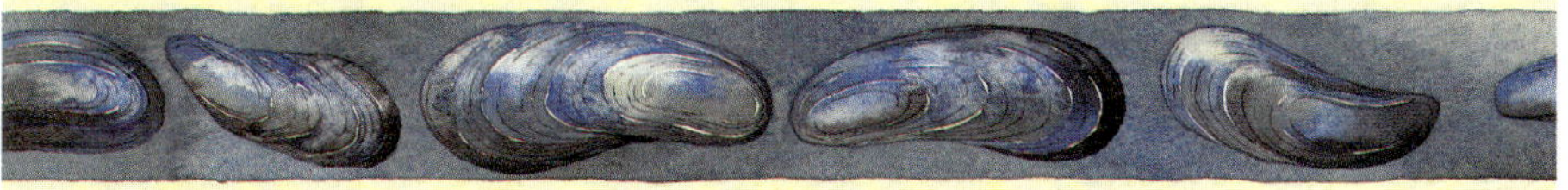

main attraction (although the fish is said to be sweet). The poisoned diner suffers paralysis during which they are often aware of what is going on around them but they can't move or speak.

There are some cases where the victim recovers from this paralysis, so the family of a man or woman who has died of fugu poisoning tend to wait for a few days before burying them, just in case.

THE EXPRESSION, 'TO EAT HUMBLE-PIE' derived from 'umble pye', a dish made from the internal organs (umbles) of the deer. This was eaten by the aristocracy in England until at least the eighteenth century, after this date it seems to have lost favour.

Later umble pies were made from livers, hearts and kidneys and were regarded as food for the poor. So while 'umbles' and 'humble' have different etymologies, the similarity in the words probably explains why having to undergo a humiliating experience is 'to eat humble-pie'.

The leek is the national emblem of Wales worn on St. David's Day. It all started in AD 640 during the battle between the Welsh, led by King Cadwallader and the Saxons. The Welsh fighters wore leeks in their caps so they could identify each other.

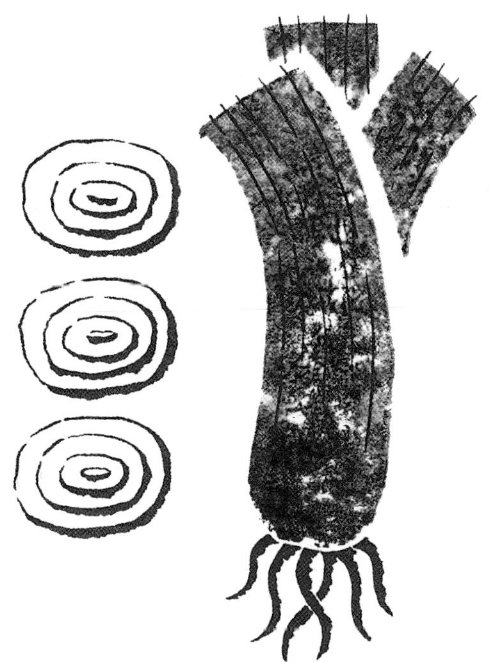

N NORTHERN CHINA some tea was drunk during the Han period (206BC - AD221), but it didn't become the beverage of the people until the late Tang period (c. 800). The Chinese took tea seriously, connoisseurs insisted that the water used to make it should come from a special place near the mouth of the Yangtze, and that it should be drunk only from porcelain cups.

The Dutch were introduce to tea, imported from India, in about 1610. They soon became great tea-drinkers, drinking as many as 100 cups a day. Even those who were ill were advised to drink 50 cups a day. From about 1720, tea began to gain favour in England and a century later many English industrial workers were living largely on bread and tea.

When the tea bag was invented in the United States, it changed tea drinking forever — tea lost its ritual quality, and became, like instant coffee, a quick drink, rather than an excuse for a tea break. In 1904 at the St Louis World's Fair, iced tea was seen in the United States for the first time, and it is still far more popular in America than hot tea.

The English novelist George Orwell called tea

'the Englishman's opium'.

A
VOCADOS WERE PLANTED in the United States in about 1833, but commercial growing didn't begin until the turn of the century. They were probably introduced to England by sailors who brought them back from their voyages (they

were originally called 'midshipman's butter'), but it wasn't until the 1960s that they became popular. Then they were available everywhere and were usually served as a first course, cut in half with a spoonful of prawn cocktail in the centre, or with vinaigrette. In California the avocado is ubiquitous: it is served in salads, as a spread, and most often in guacamole, the famous Mexican dip.

In France, avocados were available from as early as 1919. One Paris grocer stocked them all year round, so he must have had suppliers in both hemispheres. Despite having the right climate for growing them, avocados didn't appear in Australian shops in any great number until the 1960s. Now Australians use them freely — sliced in salads, mashed onto bread instead of butter in chicken sandwiches and as guacamole. In Brazil, avocados are eaten as a dessert, sprinkled with sugar.

B RILLAT-SAVARIN, AUTHOR OF THE NINETEENTH-CENTURY CLASSIC, *The Physiology of Taste*, called truffles 'black diamonds' and they are among the most rare and expensive foods in the world. They are rare because they cannot be cultivated — they grow under certain trees — or they don't, depending on the weather, the terrain, and it seems, on the truffle's whim. Truffles are hunted rather than harvested. They grow underground and you need a fine nose to detect them. That's why pigs or dogs are used; they are trained from an early age to recognise the scent. But when they home in on a truffle, they have to be restrained because truffles are fragile and must not be damaged if they are to fetch a high price on the market.

Truffles vary in weight between 20g (2/3 oz) and 200g (7 oz). There are three main types: *Périgord*, which are black inside and out; so called 'cook's truffles', which are black on the outside and white within; and *Alba* or *Piedmont* truffles, which are entirely white. In recent years agronomists have given serious consideration to commercial truffle cultivation. But since they are still not available in our supermarkets, it is to be supposed that there is more work to be done.

Published by MQ Publications Limited
254-258 Goswell Road, London EC1V 7EB

ISBN: 1-897954-05-0

1 3 5 7 9 0 8 6 4 2

Printed and bound in Italy